FLUENT WRITING

FLUENT
WRITING

How to Teach
the Art of Pacing

Denise Leograndis

Foreword by
Barry Lane

HEINEMANN
PORTSMOUTH, NH

Heinemann

A division of Reed Elsevier Inc.
361 Hanover Street
Portsmouth, NH 03801–3912
www.heinemann.com

Offices and agents throughout the world

© 2006 by Denise Leograndis

The author and publisher wish to thank those who have generously given permission to reprint borrowed material:

"Super Dad" by Aakash Patel. Reprinted by permission of New Standards.

Library of Congress Cataloging-in-Publication Data
Leograndis, Denise.
  Fluent writing : how to teach the art of pacing / by Denise Leograndis.
      p.   cm.
  Includes bibliographical references and index.
  ISBN 0-325-00826-4 (alk. paper)
  1. English language—Composition and exercises—Study and teaching (Elementary).
2. Style, Literary—Study and teaching (Elementary).   I. Title.

LB1576.L446 2006
372.62'3—dc22   2005033804

Editor: Lois Bridges
Production: Patricia Adams
Typesetter: Publishers' Design and Production Services, Inc.
Cover design: Judy Arisman
Manufacturing: Jamie Carter

Printed in the United States of America on acid-free paper
10   09   08   07   06   RRD   1   2   3   4   5

To my students, past, present and future—
You inspire me.

Contents

Foreword

Writing and Reading: Together at Last
by Barry Lane

There have been many published professional books on how to teach writing in the last twenty years. Some focus on creating a writer's workshop where students guide their own learning; others focus on teaching grammatical skills in context, or studying writing with an eye toward the writer's craft. Many of these books cite, as their goal, the need to create classrooms of fluent writers in which ideas are artistically expressed with care and detail, as opposed to formulaic textbook approaches where details march stolidly across the page obedient to their topic sentence. Until now, fluency was something writing teachers assumed grew from the knowledge of craft and process. Can we really teach fluency on its own? Denise Leograndis thinks so and, in the book you now hold in your hands, she convinced me.

Fluent Writing: How to Teach the Art of Pacing is the first professional, teacher-oriented book I know that shows that (what we call) "the flow" can be modeled, studied, taught, and learned by young writers. Early in the book Denise Leograndis tells us she is not a writer, and, although you wouldn't know it from the eloquent text she has crafted, it's clear that her passion is teaching and observing—both her own students and the work of other teachers and professional writers. She is a keen observer with a laser-sharp focus. She knows how to uncover a problem, define it, mull over ways of teaching it, and give direct guidance for building elegant minilessons that teach writing fluency at both the big level of ideas and narrative flow and the small level of sentence structure.

What I love best about *Fluent Writing* is how the author celebrates the reading–writing connection with examples of both student and published work. For a recent reading convention in Wisconsin where the theme was *Writing and Reading: Together at Last,* I wrote a comic parable that described reading and writing as brother and sister who were separated after the war. Reading went to live with her old Aunt Basal who made her answer the questions at the end of the chapter. Writing was sent away to Mr. Warriner's boarding school to formulate his ideas into five-paragraph themes. In my story, Reading suffers a mental breakdown. A billion-dollar hospital is built for her, where she is chained to a bed mouthing meaningless phrases that flash across the ceiling from dawn till dusk. She is a prisoner of the National Reading Panel and the mad scientist, Dr. Read Tiger. At the end of the story, Writing escapes from boarding school, and with the help of the 6-Trait gang from Oregon, rescues Reading and nurses her back to health by telling her "real" stories.

Reading *Fluent Writing* confirmed the meaning of my silly parable. The best way to rescue children from mindless phonic-based approaches to teaching reading is to focus on what makes writing successful. Great writing wants to be read. Great reading wants to be imitated. The pace of a novel or essay is first felt by the reader; then the writer shows up to dissect what works and repeat it in his own work. Not far behind the writer comes a master teacher like Denise Leograndis. She shows us how the magic is done, and how we can help our students replicate it in their own work, and she does it in an artful way that draws us into the process.

There is a movement, a pace, to all writing, even professional books. The pace of this book is just right.

Acknowledgments

I have heartfelt and special thanks for so many. This book would not have happened without the support of all of these fine people:

Katharine Davies Samway, literacy professor and author, you first introduced me to teaching writing and reading in a workshop way. It was your deep understanding and teaching by modeling that encouraged me to first start implementing writing workshop. And, of course, I am indebted to you for believing I could write a book, when I was almost too afraid to try.

Lois Bridges, my most wonderful and supportive editor, who believed in me and encouraged me throughout this entire process. Like a good teacher, you guided me back to the right path when I didn't see I was straying. You always pointed out my strengths and gently guided me from my weaknesses. You helped me be the best I could be.

Sheryl Dugan, literacy specialist extraordinaire, from my beginnings in learning to teach writing, you've always been there for me—patient, thoughtful, helpful in my "deep dives" toward understanding.

Polly McBride, I am sure there is no more supportive principal anywhere. You planted the seed by announcing to visiting teachers that I would write a book someday. Seemed impossible then.

My students of Room 18, during the 2004–2005 schoolyear; the year I was writing on weekends while teaching you on weekdays—your support, efforts, and encouragement were beyond your years.

To all my students, thank you for allowing me to share your wonderful writing in this book. Thank you to the parents as well. This book is not possible without all of you.

Susan Hull, colleague, friend, and neighbor, teacher of my child, reader of my drafts, you were always supportive, insightful, and encouraging. You were there for me when I needed convincing that my crisis of confidence was just part of the writing process.

Teachers at Ponderosa: Lynn Hayes, Cheryl Lopes-Coe, Cindy Pitcher, Dayna Mallobox, as well as Ellen Haas, literacy consultant, and Audrey Poppers and Brenda Wallace of the Noyce Foundation—you all were willing to read an early draft and take the time to give feedback. Your thoughtful comments helped clear the way to better writing. And your encouragement kept me going.

Meg Jackson and Chris Atchison, you were so kind to offer support and test lessons in your fifth grade class.

My husband and son, I especially owe thanks to you. You gave me emotional support and tech support as well as the precious gift of time.

Hongjian and the Wang family, thank you for caring for my child as your own so often especially when I was pushing to finish and needed the quiet.

My team of readers, my "response group"—Cece Derr, Diana Purucker, Kathy Morgan, Sheryl Dugan, Susan Hull, Dayna Mallobox—your comments were always right on. You reaffirmed my thoughts on revisions; you pointed out what I had missed. Your insightful attention to teacher details was invaluable.

And there are many, many others—friends, colleagues, neighbors, extended family—thank you for always having a smile for me and asking "How's the book coming?" Now, finally, it's done.

Introduction

I don't consider myself a writer. I am a teacher with something to share.

This book came from my desire to figure out how to teach something that I knew nothing about: pacing. There it is sitting all by itself in the narrative writing, third grade, National Center on Education and the Economy (NCEE) New Standards:

- provides pacing

Looking like we should know what it is. I looked all around for a book on the subject but I found nothing. So I started digging for a definition, an understanding I could teach from. I found bits and pieces, here and there.

I am a "go-deep" teacher, I am told. A highly reflective teacher, I am told. I love to engage in conversations with colleagues, trying to figure things out; what exactly is this concept we are trying to teach and how do we best teach it? I love to read and implement and reflect, always trying to improve my practice. Often, I am still trying to figure things out in the morning, before the bell rings, while stirring my coffee. Reflection takes time. You do it when you can.

So when the question about pacing first came up—as in "What is it and how do we teach it?"—I read and implemented and reflected and engaged in conversations and reflected some more and eventually, after years, synthesized an understanding and a basis for teaching well-crafted writing through pacing.

A Little About Myself and My School

As I am writing this introduction, it is summertime and school starts in two weeks. It will be my fourth year as an exemplar writing teacher for our six-district and growing literacy initiative sponsored by the Noyce Foundation: *www.noyce fdn.org*

My school is culturally diverse. Over twenty-one languages are spoken at our school. And because of where the school is located, feeding from adjacent but different neighborhoods, we are diverse socioeconomically as well, with about 36 percent of our students qualifying for the free or reduced-cost lunch program. Parent education levels range from completion of third grade to doctorates.

And while this is not a book on teaching English language learners, these students are part of my school and classroom population so I have included in Chapter 11 my thoughts on the matter and student writing examples and my commentary. Throughout this book are more of my thoughts on teaching our language learners in context of examples I have for you.

How to Use This Book

Read it in order. Part Two has the lessons. Please don't start there. You can't teach what you don't understand. Start here, in Part One. I've been deliberate about the path I have built for you.

But if you're the kind of reader who skips ahead, like I do, looking to pull out a simplified, condensed thought, the answer to the who-done-it, I'll save you the time. Here it is in a nutshell: Fluent writing reads fluently because it is paced well.

And from Part Two, Chapter 6, Presenting Pacing to Your Students:

We know when music sounds good, when colors look right on a canvas, and when writing reads well. Good writing has a flow, a balance, a rhythm that our brains appreciate. Writing reads well when it's paced well.

There you go. Now let's move to Chapter 1 to see how I came up with this.

Toward Building an Understanding

Synthesizing a Definition

When I first saw that NCEE New Standards bullet—*provides pacing*—I checked my memory for any knowledge of pacing in writing. Nothing. Apparently I had either forgotten or never heard of it in a writing context. I was careful to check way back to memories of lessons in my high school and college writing classes. Still nothing.

I proceeded to search out a definition. I found many similar and different and overlapping references. Eventually, I synthesized all these references and my supporting inquiry work into something that, I believe, makes sense and more importantly works well for my students.

Checking My Schema

As with any new learning that we encounter, we start building an understanding based on what we already know. As I had no pacing in writing connection, I checked my own schema for any references to *pace* and *pacing*. I found *pace car, pace yourself, set the pace, pick up the pace,* and memories of my track coach hollering at me over his stopwatch.

All references to controlling speed.

Let's look at the ubiquitous "Pace yourself." We use it in all sorts of different situations. We pace ourselves when we take on projects. For our students, we pace individual lessons and our yearlong plans. To pace something well is complex. To get the overall plan to work, you've got to consider and have control over all the details, big and small.

Control over all the details, big and small, to control the pace. True in life. Also true in writing?

I started asking around.

Advice from Others

"You know, short, medium, and long sentences," a veteran teacher told me. I nodded. I had (and still do) read plenty of student writing where each sentence ends predictably at the same length as the last. Lifeless writing. Droning writing. Certainly sentence length is a critical element for the writer to control.

So I had the specific detail of sentence length. But is that the only detail that controls the pacing in writing? I needed more.

I asked a literacy coach. "It's spending time on the important moment in the piece," she said. Yes, I understood that. I remembered a fourth-grade student from the year before. He had spent every moment of our writing time nose down, writing and writing. By the time I conferred with him, he had nine pages of meticulous details of a five-hour plane ride he took to visit a relative he rarely saw. He recounted his journey from the car ride to the airport parking lot, to the ticket counter to the takeoff, the meal, the movie, everything. The joyous two-day reunion with the relative got one short paragraph. Followed by a "The End." Boring writing. Disappointing writing.

Now I had two ways to focus a pacing lens on a piece: a small lens—controlling the pace through the details of sentence length and a big lens—the balance of proper attention and time spent on the important moments in a piece. Anything else? I kept searching.

References in Professional Books

I gathered every professional book I owned or could borrow. I scanned the indexes, tables of contents and read every possible paragraph where pacing might show up. I found a little help here and there.

Craft Lessons, *by Ralph Fletcher and JoAnn Portalupi (1998)*
In the index, under *H* for "How to Pace a Story," grades K–2. There is a lesson on page 28 where you teach "slowing things down and stretching things out."

This seemed to add some depth to the big pacing focus of balancing a piece with time spent on the important event or moment.

In the Middle, *by Nancie Atwell (1998)*

In the index, I found "pace, in fiction" on page 399. Listed are seven elements of fiction, one of which is pace:

> How quickly or slowly does the writer move the plot? Pace involves keeping a balance between *too fast* to be involving or plausible and *too* slow to hold a reader's interest.

> *Controlling speed again. But in the big pacing way—she specifically refers to balance. Balance in the plot. A matter, again, of the writer organizing the flow of events in a piece.*

After the End, *by Barry Lane (1993)*

Love the Barry! His teachings about snapshots (writing in sharp physical detail), thoughtshots (internal monologue), and exploded moments (providing many precise details to slow an important moment) have made it possible for me to help my students' writing soar. I didn't find *pacing* in his table of contents or index, but there is a reference I happened upon in Chapter 14 under "Spin-offs" on page 192:

> *Long sentence, short sentence.* Writers often learn pacing instinctively through their reading, but teachers can help by pointing out the rhythm of sentences.

He then suggests an exercise where teachers have their students write a short horror scene using several long sentences to create the tension and suspense, followed by a short one to scare the reader.

> *This adds more to the small pacing focus in controlling sentence length. He used the word* rhythm. *Rhythm of sentences. And he reminds us that reading and writing are inseparable. And there is something more he is alluding to: matching pacing strategies to the content of the piece.*

Reviser's Toolbox, *by Barry Lane (1999)*

No listing for *pacing*. But I checked in Barry's Chapter 4, Playing with Time. He has a list of eighteen lessons with titles like: "Slow Motion Moments," "Time as a Writer," "Building Scenes," and "Suspenseful Moments."

> *After looking through Barry's lessons and rereading Nancy Atwell's explanation—"How quickly or slowly does the writer move the plot"—I would*

say Barry's Chapter 4 is about pacing. Big pacing. Controlling the flow of the
story through all his listed strategies.

6 + 1 Traits of Writing, *by Ruth Culham (2003)*

Pacing is referred to under *organization trait*. On page 71, I found:

> Pacing—speeding up for wide angle and slowing down for close-ups—
> should be under control.

And on page 86, a teacher who is assessing an essay for pacing needs to keep
in mind that:

> A hallmark of a well-organized piece is that just the right amount of time
> is spent on each idea, and then the writer moves on, building to the most
> important point. . . .

*That's big pacing. And another reference to a well-paced piece as a well-
organized piece. And our first reference to pacing used outside of the narrative
genre.*

> *Knowing now about small pacing, I also looked at what Culham has to say
> about sentence length or rhythm in sentences. She's got it all under sentence flu-
> ency and word choice traits. It's not labeled pacing, but it's there. Without at-
> tention to pacing in small ways, big pacing will not read well.*

What's on the Net?

There's the axiom "consider the source." Always good advice, but when comparing information gleaned from the Net as opposed to say, a book, I would
prefer "judge the message, not the medium of conveyance." So I surfed and I
judged. I was determined to find definitions and explanations that made sense
and would be helpful.

What I found was a door into a different perspective. As a teacher slogging
away daily as best I can in an elementary classroom, it was interesting and fascinating to read about writing written for adult writers, rather than for teachers. And written by writers rather than teacher educators. I read for hours and
hours, deepening my writing knowledge pool.

However, while I enjoyed reading through all the websites on writing, I was
not getting a lot of help on pacing exactly, as many websites assumed in their

discussions that you "the reader" already understood the term. Finally, I found some help in the form of an online writer's magazine. At *www.fictionfactor.com /guests/pacing.html* I found an article in "Fiction Factor: The Online Magazine for Fiction Writers." Dr. Vicky Hinze writes:

> For a moment, let's pretend that the words we write on the page are sounds. If all the sounds are the same, then we have monotone. . . .
>
> Pacing is the rhythm of the novel, of the chapters and scenes and paragraphs and sentences. It's also the rate at which the reader reads, the speed at which novel events occur and unfold. It's using specific word choices and sentence structure—scene, chapter, and novel structure—to tap the emotions of the reader so that the reader feels what the writer wants the reader to feel at any given time during the story.

> *That's a lot. So here's a source that looks at pacing in both big and small ways, not just one or the other. And she speaks of controlling the rhythm of the writing from the overall structure, to sentence structure, down to individual word choice. "Tapping the emotions of the reader." I wondered, Does anyone else look at pacing with the big and small lenses combined? And I found "emotions of the reader" intriguing. Pacing as a way to tap the emotions of the reader . . . that deserves more thought.*

I surfed my way to the Frostburg State University English Department, in Frostburg, Maryland, at *www.frostburg.edu/clife/writingcenter/techniq.htm* where I found:

> Pacing: Sentences should be consistent with the subject matter. Generally, longer sentences are appropriate for more leisurely and serious topics. They slow down the reader. Short sentences convey action or tenseness. Manipulating sentence length, then, helps you establish the appropriate pace for your writing. By coupling changing sentence lengths with a variety of sentence openings, a writer can avoid boring the reader. Variety is the spice of writing; proper pacing provides the spice.

> *Here we're back to sentence length but it's more complicated than just varying the lengths. It's what Barry alluded to—you need to manipulate your sentence structure according to your content—and that makes sense——to write is to understand your purpose; there should be decidedly different purposes, depending on content, that require different ways to control the pacing. Dr. Hinze's "Tapping the emotions of the reader" could be applied here. I began to see that*

pacing strategies in sentence length, structure, and word choice help the writer scare a reader in a horror piece, surprise a reader in a mystery, and soothe a reader in a memoir.

Bookstore Writing Instruction

Because I loved that sojourn into the world of what writers are saying to writers (and would-be writers) about writing, and to be thorough, and in hopes of finding more, I visited my local Borders bookstore. I sat down in front of twelve shelves of books on writing in their writing instruction section. I went through every book. During my first search, I found only one reference to pacing.

Conflict, Action & Suspense, *by William Noble (1994)*
On page 58, Noble writes,

> One of the toughest writing skills to develop is a competent sense of pace, an ability to keep the story flowing smoothly even as mini-climaxes occur or events whipsaw or characterizations change.
>
> *So* flow *is still a key word. The reader will notice if your piece does not flow. That sounds like a delicate, complex combination of big and small pacing.*

More recently, in doing more research for this book, I went back to the bookstore to see if they had any new titles. I found three more references, all of them in series books.

The Everything Creative Writing Book, *by Carol Whiteley (2002)*
Here I found two references, the first on page 20:

> Still another aspect of the short story that is crucial is pacing. Because there are many fewer sentences, each must move the story forward in some way. If you take pages to describe the main character and set the scene for what will unfold, time will run out before you get to the main elements, and the reader will become impatient to discover how the issues will be resolved. Short-story writers need to jump right into their subject and keep right on going.
>
> *Short story. Certainly that's what we are dealing with. Our students are not producing novels. And she's talking about organizing the flow of the piece, the big pacing idea.*

The second reference I found is on page 26, in an interview between the book's author and writer Susan Fry where they discuss how "mystery/horror stories need a different pace than other types of writing. . . ."

Again back to content. Different content requires different pacing.

The Everything Writing Well Book, *by Pamela Rice Hahn (2003)*
On page 26, she writes,

> Pacing is the time you take to convey your information. If you do it at a slow, leisurely pace, you will create a much different impact than you will if you follow the action crisply and closely.
>
> The pacing will also depend on the kind of manuscript you're writing. As you'll see in [c]hapter 21, there are a variety of fiction and nonfiction markets. Depending on what you're writing, each type of story or book (and each type of scene) will carry with it different requirements when it comes to pacing. If you're setting up scenes, a slow pace is probably effective. As previously mentioned, in a high-action scene, you want events to unfold quickly to keep the reader at a high emotional level of involvement.

This sounds like big and small pacing combined, with the connection to emotion in the content.

And on page 257, in a discussion of the use of flashbacks, Hahn notes,

> A word of caution—never use a flashback in the middle of an important, exciting scene. You'll only detract from the emotional impact of the fast pace.

Emotional impact. Here's the emotion thing again. Yes, pacing sets the mood. I remember a conversation about pacing with literacy specialist Jennifer Gray. She talked about actually feeling trapped inside the setting—a house—of a horror novel she was reading; the pacing was such that she felt like she could barely breathe and she just wanted out of that house. Of course all she had to do was put the book down but what fun is that? I loved her point about her breathing. Exactly. Our breathing is affected by the way the writer has crafted the pacing of his or her piece. Different pacing, different feelings, different breathing. Thanks, Jennifer, this was the beginning of a powerful tool I use to help my students understand what pacing means to a reader. I ask them to pay attention to my breathing as I read to them, to pay attention to their own breathing as they read, to pay attention to the breathing they create for their reader in their own writing.

I found one last reference in a series book with a title that elicits confidence: *The Complete Idiot's Guide to Writing a Novel* by Tom Monteleone (2004). Tom writes:

> When writers and editors talk about the pace of a novel, they're concerned with the flow of information and how it reaches the reader.
> Different speeds of delivery, word choice, and content help you control your pacing.

He's concise. That's big and small pacing. And in two sentences!

Taking My Growing Understanding Back to the NCEE New Standards

How could the NCEE standards include provides pacing *as a required standard element and not say enough about it so that teachers could understand what it is we are supposed to teach? I must have missed something. I went back, armed with a wider vocabulary and understanding for where pacing might be referenced but not specifically named. In the section,* Third Grade Writing Standard 3: Language Use and Conventions, I *found*:

> [U]se varying sentence patterns and lengths to slow reading down, speed it up or create mood.

Sounds like small pacing, doesn't it?

And then in the Third Grade Narrative Writing Standards, I found:

> Creates a sequence of events that unfolds naturally.

Sounds like big pacing, doesn't it?

And this in the Fourth and Fifth Grade Narrative Account Standards:

> [U]ses a range of appropriate strategies, such as dialogue and tension or suspense.

Sounds like small pacing strategies to support big pacing.

The Definition

As I synthesized all my research, a definition was forming. It appears small pacing and big pacing work to support each other, seamlessly blending their characteristics together. The flow of the word choice and sentences, the balance of the descriptions, moments, and events, and the rhythm in a piece need to combine smoothly in both big and small ways to effectively control this really complex, multilayered thing called pacing.

I wanted a definition that covers all that pacing is, big and small, keeping the complex meaning without being lengthy, using as few words as possible without being overly concise and therefore inaccurate. It was tough. But here it is:

Pacing is all that makes the flow, the balance, the rhythm of writing.

That about covers it. Pacing is huge. It's also basic and essential to good writing. Obviously, this definition would only be a starting point for your instruction. My definition is not enough by itself; it requires explanation and discussion. The next step to prepare to teach our developing writers is to look in children's literature and actually be able to identify pacing.

2

Seeing Pacing in Mentor Texts

After all that research and synthesis, we have a working definition of *pacing*:

> *Pacing is all that makes the flow, the balance, the rhythm of the writing.*

It's time for a test drive.

Back to the Classroom Library

Defining *pacing* is one thing. Learning to recognize it in writing is another.

After synthesizing the definition, I took the definition and my new understanding to my classroom library, to see if I could find pacing strategies. Inquiry work.

I looked for help from some of my favorite authors. I looked for big and small pacing in picture books by Jane Yolen and Cynthia Rylant, Tony Johnston and Jonathan London. I looked for big and small pacing in chapter books by Barbara Parks and Gary Paulsen, Jerry Spinelli and Orson Scott Card. Could I recognize pacing in their writing? Could I point it out to myself and others? Slowly at first. With a lot of reflection and rereading, I was gradually able to see how the writer built the fluency, the pacing, into his or her writing. I applied my inquiry work to my lessons and guided inquiry work with my students who started to notice more ways to build and control pacing in a piece. Together, over time, we learned.

Now I can't help taking a pacing lens to writing everywhere. To *Newsweek*, to Hemingway, to blogs. As I continue to notice new ways that competent writers cleverly, brilliantly control the pacing in their works (and how incompetent writers don't), my understanding continues to deepen. I am amazed at the power of pacing in writing. And now I understand—if writing is done well, if it reads fluently, then it's well paced. So simple. So complex.

Exploring Favorite Books

Let's use just the small pacing lens first and have a look at some of my favorite children's books. For now, we'll be looking mostly at the rhythm and flow of the sentence structure and word choice, but also the content in those sentences, because we know from our research that those elements work together.

Cynthia Rylant

Many of us use Cynthia Rylant's writing to teach from, let's start there. Here is just the first page of her picture book *The Relatives Came* (1993).

> It was in the summer of the year when the relatives came. They came up from Virginia. They left when their grapes were nearly purple enough to pick, but not quite.

Read it aloud. Notice your relaxed breathing. Rylant has created a thoughtful mood, delivered to the reader's ear by deliberate pacing controlled through the flow and the rhythm of her carefully crafted sentence length and structure. Notice the two prepositional phrases in a row in the first sentence, "in the summer of the year." Rhythmic. Notice the soft flow of first the longer, then shorter, then longer sentence. Notice how the third sentence closes the set of three with the independent clause following the comma. A slight hold in your breath. Everything flows together as an invitation to read it slowly, melodically.

How would it sound if she had chosen a different pace? What if it were a quicker, almost urgent pace? It might read like this:

> They were coming, the relatives. Up from Virginia. The grapes could wait. They weren't ripe enough to pick anyway.

What did I do here to change the pace? Read it aloud. Notice your breathing. This revision requires quicker breaths. You have to manage the comma and the periods that come up faster because the sentences and clauses are shorter. Short sentences quicken the pace by demanding quicker breaths from the reader. Quicker breaths typically accompany more intense emotional responses—in this case, urgency. Something else is different, besides the shorter sentences. The content has changed. "They were coming, the relatives" sounds like an urgent announcement, whereas, "It was in the summer of the year when the relatives came," sounds like a soft reflection. An urgent story is not the tale that Cynthia Rylant wanted to convey to her reader. Rylant shows us that the pacing itself helps to tell the tale. She controls it beautifully, through her conventions, her craft, and her content.

Orson Scott Card

Let's look at the pacing in a different type of book and a different reading level. A chapter book for young adults.

In fifth grade, my son discovered the prolific writings of award-winning author, Orson Scott Card. I was worried that a ten-year-old, even a precocious one, might not be able to comprehend young adult writing, so I offered to read and discuss the books with him. What a treat for me! We started with Card's first science fiction novel, *Ender's Game* (2002). I could not put that book down. I was up way past midnight every night on an exhilarating, page-turning ride. Card held a fast pace from beginning to end, all 324 pages. How did he do it? When I was finished reading and enjoying it the first time through, I went back to study his use of craft, how the craft connected to the content and his use of conventions.

Using the small pacing lens, let's just have a look at page 1. He opens his book with a conversation. Read it aloud. Notice your breathing.

> "I've watched through his eyes, I've listened through his ears, and I tell you he's the one. Or at least as close as we're going to get."
>
> "That's what you said about the brother."
>
> "The brother tested out impossible. For other reasons. Nothing to do with his ability."
>
> "Same with the sister. And there are doubts about him. He's too malleable. Too willing to submerge himself in someone else's will."
>
> "Not if the other person is his enemy."
>
> "So what do we do? Surround him with enemies all the time?"
>
> "If we have to."
>
> "I thought you said you liked this kid."
>
> "If the buggers get him, they'll make me look like his favorite uncle."
>
> "All right. We're saving the world, after all. Take him."

The reader doesn't quite know who is doing the speaking until a few chapters in. And it's difficult to know what and whom they are talking about. What a writer leaves out is just as significant as what he or she puts in. Leaving out this bit of content—identification and description of the speakers—creates an intense and secretive mood. Yet the content that is presented is plenty to engage you as a reader—you have a mystery to solve, and you want to solve it because the dialogue is crafted in such a compelling manner with lines such as " . . . saving the world, after all. Take him." which draw you in even more. Look at the sentence structure. It's short, brisk, including a fragment—"For other reasons." The sentence structure supports the intensity. There is no relaxed breathing here.

What if the author had started his book out this way:

> "I've watched through his eyes, I've listened through his ears, and I tell you he's the one. Or at least as close as we're going to get," said Colonel Graff emphatically.
>
> The Colonel was a tall man with slightly graying temples and deeply traced lines of the weight of the future of the world etched into his somber face. He wore his military uniform stiffly, with the pride of many generations. As he and the Major sat in the spartan military office, the setting sun offered its final rays through olive-green curtains waving quietly in the evening's dying breeze.

For Card, this pace would kill the story he wants to tell. He knows character identification and descriptions and bits of setting can be added concisely, surgically, and only as absolutely necessary so as to maintain the pace appropriate to an intense plot. The long sentence structure together with the descriptive content serves to slow the pace. (Although, in the lessons section of this book, we'll see that a long sentence structure can also be crafted to be intense, depending on content, conventions, and word choice.) Like Rylant, Card shows us that the pace itself helps to tell the tale. He controls it purposefully.

Jane Yolen

Let's move back to picture books. One of my favorite books to teach from is Jane Yolen's *Owl Moon* (1987). I love the first page; it starts out beautifully, "It was late one winter night, long past my bedtime," followed by a description of the farm setting in vivid sensory detail.

Yolen's attention to small pacing provides readers with a lyrical, flowing, soft and slow beginning. Gracefully written. We are gently pulled in to join daughter and dad's owling experience.

But what if she had intended a different pace, an intense pace to go out and find that owl? It might read more like the start of Card's *Ender's Game*:

> "I've been watching the weather. I've been watching the moon. Tonight is the best chance we're going to get."
> "That's what you said last time."
> "Yeah. I was wrong. I'm right tonight."
> "I hear a train."
> "Ignore it. You ready?"
> "Ready, Pa."
> "All right. Let's find that owl."

Ridiculous. This is not the story that Jane Yolen wanted to tell. Through her small pacing strategies—her craft and convention choices that support her content—she offers us a gentle story. Like Rylant and Card, Yolen has also shown us that the pace itself helps to tell the tale. She controls it masterfully.

By comparing and contrasting these examples, we can see that writers purposefully control pacing in small ways. We know, from our definition, that controlling the pacing of a piece is multilayered. What about big pacing? Controlling the flow and balance of story elements—setting, character, plot, and resolution. In my research I found that small and big pacing work together. So, what does that look like in our mentor texts?

The Small Supports the Big

In looking at big pacing, we look at the flow and balance across the entire story, the speed at which story elements are presented, how long the writer stays with each element, and the speed at which the story unfolds.

Cynthia Rylant

Let's look again at *The Relatives Came*. You will need to get a copy of the text and look at the whole story. Focus now with the big lens. How did she do it? There is no place in this picture book where you feel things are moving too slowly or too fast, for example, staying with a setting description too long, or not enough character development. It's a story of family togetherness to be savored. The scenes are slowed with descriptive content crafted with vivid detail—the hugging, the breathing, the relatives' arms and legs over each other while sleeping at night.

Even the time-compressed parts have a slowness to them. Rylant begins the story with time compression—compacting the relatives' long drive from Virginia into a few sentences, yet the time-compressed sentences keep a slowness through the use of precise detail in the description of the consumed pop, crackers, and sandwiches. You've seen time compression that does not appear leisurely: "the next day," "after a month," "early next year." Even though Rylant has compressed some parts of the story, she holds the lovely, reflective mood throughout her entire piece with carefully crafted small pacing. Without attention to the small pacing, the overall big pacing would not have the same effect.

It is difficult to separate big and small pacing. But it appears the craft in the small supports the umbrella of the big. Not the other way around. A writer could spend the right amount of time on each element—the character development, the setting(s)—unfolding the plot, as appropriate to the content, but if the small pacing doesn't sing, the whole thing falls flat.

Orson Scott Card

In Card's novel, *Ender's Game*, his small pacing strategies also support the big, overall pacing. Every chapter begins with an intense dialogue-only scene. These intense scenes are part of the organizational structure; they help to pull the reader along quickly through the book.

Looking closely at *Ender's Game* again, looking for small pacing craft, for what Card did to move the big pacing along at such a rapid speed, I chose this typical example:

> Ender felt sick. He had only meant to catch the boy's arm. No. No, he had meant to hurt him, and had pulled with all his strength. He hadn't meant it to be so public, but the boy was feeling exactly the pain Ender had meant him to feel. Null gravity had betrayed him, that was all. I am Peter. I'm just like him. And Ender hated himself.

Intense content of violence, self-doubt, and loathing. With short sentence structure, simple grammar, and simple word choice, Card has his reader breathing quick and choppy like his character must be in this internal monologue. He could have written this paragraph using small pacing craft like longer sentences with more complicated word choice and structure, but that would have slowed things down for the reader, slowed the breathing and the emotion, slowed the unfolding of the story. In his big pacing, Card spends most of his time in the story elements of plot and character development with minimal time spent in setting descriptions. But as he takes the reader through these big pacing elements, he keeps things moving along with deliberate small pacing strategies. His small pacing supports the big pacing—the speed at which his story unfolds—fast—all the way to page 324.

Jane Yolen

In *Owl Moon,* Yolen chooses not to rip her reader through her tale. Her story is soft and quiet; no dialogue, other than owl calls, until the very end. She offers the reader places to linger in her big pacing choices, taking time through small pacing strategies of careful word choice and precise descriptive detail to unfold her setting and character descriptions, slowly unfolding her plot in all the time it takes to walk through the woods and call repeatedly to the owl before she freezes the story in time and allows the reader the chance to enjoy every slow moment of the actual sighting. Her word choice, her sentence structure, her craft in her small pacing supports the big, overall pace of the story.

Controlling pacing is complicated and multilayered. As teachers, we need to unravel this complicated structure by using familiar texts so that our students can develop an understanding of pacing and then learn to craft pacing in their own writing.

Beginning to Think About My Teaching

Learning to recognize pacing, big and small, in writing is one thing. Breaking it down and organizing it into a teaching plan is a bit like wrestling an octopus. I needed an organized plan so I could teach my students pacing, help them understand the definition, help them notice pacing strategies, label the strategies and apply them to their own writing, and provide scaffolding and a foundation for them to construct meaning. But it was difficult pinning it all down. How do you simplify something so huge, complex, and multilayered? Let's set aside the mentor texts for a moment and think about what we know.

Three Main Components of Pacing

A piece of writing can be viewed through a big pacing lens or a small one. When we look through either lens we see there is so much going on. But what we've seen can be broken into three main components: content, conventions, and craft. Go back to the start of this chapter and circle these words wherever they come up. See what I mean? The writers discussed here are using just these three things to manage the pacing, big and small. We see the writers manage pacing through

- *Content.* Is it a soft piece about relatives visiting or an urgent sci-fi novel? Content indicates the kind of pacing needed.
- *Conventions.* Used to manage the pace by controlling the way the reader will read the writing.
- *Craft.* There are so many different kinds of craft strategies or ways with words (Ray 1999). Every choice a writer makes speeds up or slows down or steadies the pace of their writing.

It is through the manipulation of these three intertwined, interdependent components that an author controls his or her pace. They are big, but at least there are just three of them.

I use the word *components* here because *elements* is used in other areas of study when talking about stories. *Components* sounds right and works well. And it provides alliteration, which helps my memory paths.

Craft. Content. Conventions.

The more I thought about it, the more I understood that I was able to identify these three components because I was already teaching them. When we teach writing, we teach craft, content, and conventions. The problem is we teach them in pieces, lots and lots of pieces. At least I did, and it wasn't working.

Thinking More About My Teaching— Pulling the Pieces Together

In fact, in my writing workshop, I was quite busy teaching the pieces: strong leads, grammar, character descriptions, punctuation, settings, purposeful dialogue, vivid word choice, simile, and so on. An endless list. I had piles of books to help me. At least I knew to refer to mentor texts to help me teach. I knew to guide my students with cues like, "What do we notice about what the author is doing? Now you try." Yet, without understanding and teaching pacing, what I started to see was I was giving my students the patches without the quilt. And it showed in their patchy writing—they learned to create beautiful similes, "gems," and they randomly stuck them in here and there. They learned to craft a detailed setting to begin their narratives, but there was no flow or purpose to tie it to the rest of the piece. They tried to vary their sentence length, a bit here, a bit there, but with no purpose that a reader needs to support the content. Their writing had no flow, no balance, no rhythm. No pacing. No wonder. I didn't know what pacing was.

I began to see that without pacing, we aren't showing students how all the pieces work together. We give them the patches without the quilt. I learned pacing is in the standards for a reason; readers expect controlled, purposeful pacing in good writing.

Eventually, I changed the way I taught writing. I began to tie everything to pacing because I had learned that everything, in good writing, *is* tied to pacing.

It worked. Understanding writing got easier for my students. Tying everything they did in their writing to pacing gave them one firm, overarching concept to hold onto as they wrote. As I spoke to the group or conferred with a student, I could talk about how the content in their piece, or a certain craft strategy or use of conventions they were working on affected the flow or the balance or the rhythm of their piece. It was the help they needed to understand, to tie the pieces together, to make sense of it all, and most important, to improve.

We still discussed pieces. Lots and lots of pieces. But we would always step back and ask how each bit supported the pacing. Was everything working together? We were always looking back to the purpose behind the drafting and revision choices they were making. Always asking, how will the writing sound to the reader?

I now teach writing through pacing beginning early in the year. I help my students look at our mentor texts and their own writing through the big and small pacing lenses. By the middle and latter part of the school year if I say, "The pacing is off," heads nod in complex understanding.

How much better can your students do through this looking-at-everything-through-pacing plan? Heaps, I believe. I believe that writing well is a skill that can be learned through orderly analysis and guided meaning construction. I have seen my more logical, "good at math" students, do very well; writing is not just about the pieces, it's about how they can engineer the pieces together in all sorts of interesting big and small ways. My English learners end up writing far better than they can speak. And all my students rise to the high expectations, standing on the everything-in-writing-is-tied-to-pacing scaffold, following the clear path of meaning construction, each at their own speed.

The most difficult students to teach, I usually find, are the ones who come with the label *writer*. What they typically have is that little extra elusive something called talent, which makes them potential artists on paper. Unfortunately, I find it takes awhile for them to want to really listen and learn, to really see a mentor text for what it is: a wonderful tool, a door to lead them to understand what writing can be. They think they know writing already and it takes extra time for them to see there is so much they don't know. That they need to let go of the multiple flowery adjectives, extravagant similes, and other unpurposeful fluff that may make their writing appear, at first glance, "writerly" when what they actually have are just some loosely strung together overworked pieces. Learning pacing strategies in particular helps these students who need to start seeing they have patches of inflated prose, no quilt, no fluent piece of writing.

When you have a child who is ready to listen to the fluency of writing when you read aloud to the class, to absorb the wonder of the craft in what they hear and read on their own, and when they write to think outside themselves and of the reader, then you have a writer in the making. Most every child can learn to write well. It's a skill, not a talent. We just need to make writing a learnable, enjoyable, doable endeavor. What I found, above all, is learning to write well-crafted, well-paced writing is all based on the connection to reading. Let's explore that connection further in the next chapter.

3

The Reading Connection

When we teach writing, we teach our students to "stand on the shoulders of authors" (Ray 1999). As professional teachers, we need to do the same. To acquire knowledge for the product, we study the writing of our favorite authors. To acquire knowledge to teach the process, we study the writing of our favorite teacher educators. Then we envision and we apply.

Filtered through my growing understanding of writing, of pacing, of my work with my students in my classroom, and of my own personality as a teacher, I owe this chapter to Katie Wood Ray's (1999) *Wondrous Words,* to her articulation of what it means to read like a writer.

Reading Influences Writing

We have identified *pacing* as the one overarching idea on which to hang all the pieces of our writing instruction to help our students construct meaning. Big pacing. Small pacing. Content, conventions, craft. When we study the writing of fine authors we see there are an infinite number of ways to craft a well-paced piece. There are nuances in "ways with words" (Ray 1999) that create the sound of well-written language, the small pacing. And there are vast considerations for structural organization, the big pacing. I can't identify everything, and I can't teach everything, especially in just one school year. And even if all our grade levels got together and agreed—OK, you take simile and metaphor, we'll take close echo and artful use of *and* (Ray 1999), you take flashbacks and we'll take the story-within-a-story structure, and so on—each student would still only learn a fraction of all there is to learn about writing well. Our best hope is to give our students the power to teach themselves, every day, every time they pick up a book. Of course they are being influenced by the sounds and structure of language every time they read, but it is our job as teachers to explicitly guide and heighten their understanding. We don't have to look far to find evidence that professional writers understand the influence of other writers upon their own work.

The connection between reading and writing is powerful. Stephen King (2000) wrote in *On Writing: A Memoir of the Craft* that "Reading is the creative center of a writer's life." Students who learn to notice the craft of what they read will take themselves beyond what teachers see and have time to teach. We need to give all our students the gift of learning to read like a writer so that they will continually grow their understanding of what good writing can be. To do that, we need to strengthen the reading connection.

This is not easy. It's developmental. It takes time. I work on it from the first day of school. "Writers understand the reading connection," I tell my students. I post quotes by famous authors around the room to prove it. My favorite, and the one I refer to most, is also from Stephen King. He calls it his "Prime Directive": "Read a lot and write a lot." (I also use it as a spell check—"See, a lot is *two* words.")

Other comments about the reading connection from authors:

> *"I learned how to write from writers. I didn't know any personally, but I read . . ."*
> —Cynthia Rylant
> *"Just read for about four years before you even start. Read everything you can get your hands on."* —Gary Paulsen speaking to a group of aspiring writers
> *"Read as much as you can. Read fifty or a hundred poems by others for every one you try to write of your own."* —Ted Kooser, U.S. Poet Laureate

It seems every author interviewed can answer the question, Which writers have most influenced your work?

Edward P. Jones won the 2004 Pulitzer Prize for his historical fiction novel, *The Known World*. He answered the previous question with a list of seven writers. He named one in particular, James Joyce, as the primary inspiration for his collection of stories *Lost in the City*, which won the PEN/Hemingway Award.

J. K. Rowling cites C. S. Lewis, E. Nesbit, and Paul Gallico as authors from her childhood who influenced her work, and Jane Austen as her favorite author of all time.

This is what people do. In any field. We learn from the work of people who come before us. No one learns in a vacuum. Our students need to see learning from *writers* as part of their learning-to-write process. It's what *writers* do, you can tell them, so that's what we're going to do. You might ask your students to consider: Is any writer's writing style really his or her own? Or is it a compilation of all he or she has read, funneled through some conscious or subconscious personality filter? "Writing is individual—It is not unique," says Katie Wood Ray (1999). Indeed. We learn and build from those that come before us.

Strategies for Enhancing the Reading Connection

There is another point about the reading connection: developing an "ear" for good writing. We can study writer's craft, label it, and apply it, but we also need to develop a sense of what good writing, fluent writing, sounds like. That "ear" is essential for understanding pacing.

I happened to catch an interview with Glenn Close on TV. I grabbed a pen and scribbled down a few things she said about the scripts for the roles she has played. This quote is as accurate as my brain and pen were fast:

> Really great writing has an innate rhythm. It makes a script easy to work with. There is music to the words.

We know writing reads well when it is well paced. We know readers expect writing to be well paced. Readers may not be able to articulate that a piece of writing is well-paced (like Glenn Close did), but they do notice when it isn't. The writing feels flat or awkward, or they get bored or feel rushed or confused.

Since pacing is a "how does it read?" and "how does it sound?" thing, the first way you teach pacing is by strengthening your students' ability to really hear what they read or what they listen to. Our students are just beginning their lives as readers and writers. They need our help.

You can enhance the reading connection to help your students learn pacing through

1. *Read-alouds.* They hear how you read a piece. This allows them to tune their ears to the pacing of the writing.

2. *Open Inquiry.* The discussions you have around a whole-class read-aloud. This helps students notice the strategies that authors use to create pacing. These discussions are open and broad in that students are encouraged to comment on anything they notice in a writer's craft. And you comment on what you notice. This type of inquiry encourages students to develop that reading like a writer skill and begin to articulate what they are noticing. It is a precursor to more focused, specific guided inquiry.

3. *Guided Inquiry.* You follow the steps of inquiry, but you guide the search. You lead the hunt to the *what* and *why* of specific craft strategies and see how they support pacing. You and your students label the strategies, think about where else you have seen them, then students envision the strategies in their own writing projects, then students apply.

4. *Independent Reading.* Students, on their own, find pacing strategies in their independent reading, and apply them purposefully in their writing. At first you can guide what you want them to notice in their independent reading, based on that day's focus lesson in your writing work. And then after a time, they will begin to notice all kinds of pacing strategies on their own.

As they gradually improve as listeners and as readers, they'll gradually improve as writers.

Read-Alouds—Hearing Pacing

We've got two sides to the same coin; all that is pacing in writing is what provides the pleasure in reading the writing. Reading, heads. Writing, tails. Inseparable. To help our students write well, we need to teach our students first to be aware of themselves in the audience-for-writing role. And even before that, before we can say, "What is it that we noticed that made us love this writing?" they need to love the writing. If you read well, and if you love writing, it will show in your voice. We want our students to become aware of both sides of the coin. Then they will begin to see that pacing matters in their own writing because an audience loves, appreciates, and expects to read well-paced writing. We want them to understand writers write for an audience—the reader—even if that reader is only themselves.

It is also important for you to read out loud because many students lack fluency. These are the students who struggle most with their writing. They need to hear fluent writing read fluently. Without fluency, when they read to themselves, how they can hear the subtleties in an author's small pacing strategies? You cannot manage small pacing through varying your sentence length if you read right through periods. You cannot hear the beauty of the pacing in the sound of the language if you read in a monotone voice. And in consideration of English language learners, you cannot control syntax for craft if you are not fluent in English syntax in the first place. We know language is learned through immersion, so immerse them. For all your students, you, the teacher, have to model good reading. Excellent reading. They need to hear the fluency; they need to hear you breathe with the book.

You can do it. You can choose books you love. You can take a deep breath and breathe with that book as you read aloud. Let your voice come from your heart. Let your students hear the art and passion that is writing.

It's not too difficult. Well-written writing in any genre is a joy to share. I don't know how many times and ways I have analyzed and dissected parts and pieces of my mentor texts. But every time I read them through, out loud to my class, I am moved. I cry, I laugh, I sigh. Well-written writing is powerful no matter how many times you've read it. How can you not be moved? Well-written writing feeds our passionate selves.

I make my read-alouds a sacred time; there is no drawing or fiddling, only absolute attention to my voice. I actually consider a read-aloud a performance. I've never said as much to my students, but they often break out in spontaneous applause after that silent savoring moment that comes at the end of a read. I'm not sure if it's me or the words they are applauding. Probably both. But they do soon learn what to say, "Wow! That book is really well crafted, let's study it!" I read Jane Yolen's *Miz Berlin Walks* with a gentle Southern accent (I visited my sister in Nashville enough times to able to do that). I read Jack Gantos' *Joey Pigza Looses Control* with all the intensity that the author intended, actually running out of breath near the end of a desperate ninety-five-word sentence. And I read Jonathan and Aaron London's *White Water* with all the changes in breathing that it requires, from soft and relaxed, to scared and urgent. When your students hear you read well, they start to hear the pacing—the flow, the balance, the rhythm—of the writing.

Reading and writing are inseparable. Although I have had more than one English teacher who didn't think so. I remember sterile classrooms, void of literature, full of grammar charts and diagrammed sentences where we students were told to write. We were largely unsuccessful. And unhappy. Well-crafted, well-paced writing? Forget it.

Yet, some time beginning after college, I remember friends commenting to me, after receiving long, reflective letters around some rite of passage point in our lives, that I wrote well. They enjoyed my letters, my writing. I certainly did not learn to write from my writing teachers. And I certainly am not a *writer* because I have not made it my life's work. There is only one explanation for the level of writing ability that I do have: my reading life. Over time and through lots of reading I transferred the sound of language to my writing.

Given time, and through lots and lots of reading, the sounds of well-crafted language will emerge in our students' writing as well. Only we don't have fifteen or twenty years to wait. Having students listen to the sounds of well-written language is just a start, a foundation. We also have to be explicit in our teaching.

Open Inquiry—Noticing Pacing

After reading well to your students, your next step is to talk informally about the writing that the class is enjoying. You begin to help them build that "habit of mind" (Ray 1999) that they need to become metacognitive learners.

You are not teaching your students to write novels, but you can teach them to appreciate pacing in chapter books. Wonderful discussions will take place—in small-group literacy study circles and in whole-class read-aloud—about big pacing and the many small pacing strategies that support it. How much time is the author spending in the different story elements: the setting descriptions, different character development, the buildup, the climax or turning point, the resolution? Why? And how is it done—what small pacing strategies do you appreciate, as a reader, that smoothly support the big pacing? We need to always go back to purpose. Always back to audience. Thoughtful reading will support good writing. Do this with your picture book read-alouds as well. These are informal whole-class discussions where you marvel at the small pacing strategies that actually changed your breathing while you read. Discuss the rhythm, the sound of the language. Discuss the big pacing strategies in the story elements—how much time was spent in setting, character development, plot development, and resolution. Ask your students if they enjoyed the big pacing choices that the author made. Why or why not? What do they think about the small pacing convention and craft choices? What about this run-on or that fragment here? How do these choices support the content? What would this part sound like if it was written differently? As teachers, you do this work to help students construct meaning so that they can apply this thinking to their own work. Ask them, "We are learning to read like writers. What is going on here in this writing that we love as readers?"

The next step is to get more explicit.

Guided Inquiry—Identifying Pacing Strategies

"Writers often learn pacing instinctively through their reading, but teachers can help by pointing out the rhythm of sentences."

—BARRY LANE, AFTER THE END (1993)

Yes, it's our job, as teachers, to point things out, things that writers do that make good writing. I get rather pointed about it.

Always with the standards in mind, always with what I see students need to work on in their writing, I am thinking about what I should specifically be focusing on in writers' craft. I am always thinking—because teaching writing is a thinking curriculum—how can I best guide my students, considering the standards and where they are in their development as writers toward meeting standards? Open inquiry is lovely, and you and your students could notice different things until the cows come home, but I do feel that time is of the essence. The purpose of the open inquiry is to show our students that they need to think about what they read, that there are strategies to be noticed. In open inquiry, you model for them how to notice writing strategies. You invite your students to notice with you. And you and your students can notice anything, it's open. In guided inquiry, you zero in and specifically guide the direction of the inquiry to what you know students need to learn next. We have student writers. We have one school year. We must be explicit.

Learning to Use Mentor Texts

It's rare that I won't have a mentor text in hand during a conference. If the student doesn't have a copy of the book they are working with, I will send them to get a particular text out of a genre mentor basket. For instance, I'll suggest to the student, "So you want to change the pace of your story here, at this point, from very slow to suddenly fast. Let's look at how Jonathan London crafts that kind of change in *White Water*." I always go back to a mentor text where the real writing instruction is.

Although I start the year with open inquiry, developing students' reading-like-writer skills, as we move along in the year I find my students are all over the place when it comes to using mentor texts to specifically help them with their writing. Even though we use our favorite texts to study the vast craft of writing well together, when it comes to independent writing time, some will use mentor texts on their own, reading alone, noticing, applying. Some students won't touch a mentor text unless I put one in their hands, and then eventually they get their own. And some, usually students new to our school, or the I-already-know-how-to-write ones, resist the concept of applying what we are learning from writers until months have past then finally, when they look up and see that everyone is becoming more and more successful using mentor texts, they get on board. Like all really complex concepts, everyone constructs meaning in their own time. As teachers, we can only continue to model, to scaffold, to nudge our students along until that time comes.

To help students get to the point where they can apply the craft they notice to their own writing, they first need a critical step of inquiry—envisioning. They need to be able to take what they have noticed and envision that craft in their own writing projects. I know I am having success, and they are beginning to internalize the envision step of inquiry when I start to hear things like: "I want to pace my beginning slowly, with lots of sensory detail like in *Owl Moon*, and I want to explode the most important moment, like the last rapid in *White Water*, and then I want to end my story using the list strategy like in *Thundercake*." There we go. That's a writer in the making. Your students will learn to think like this as you explicitly and predictably practice the steps of inquiry. And I have provided specific help for you in Part Two of this book, beginning in Chapter 8, Basic Small Pacing Lessons.

Seeing the Craft in Writing

There's just one little problem with helping students construct the bridge between the writing in mentor texts and their own writing. And I hear it mentioned every year by teachers who visit my classroom. "But you *know* what craft is, what text has what and why it's there, and you can just reach for a book and turn to a page and help your students see. All we see is the story, not the writing." Yes, but I didn't see the writing in the beginning either and I am still learning because there is so much to learn. The magic about inquiry is you don't have to know what you're looking for before you find it. You know you have to teach engaging beginnings because it's in the standards and your students' beginnings don't engage. But you are not quite sure what exactly it is in a well-crafted beginning that engages. That's OK. You just have to be willing to take a closer look. However, I know how very difficult this is, trying to identify craft in good writing, you feel like you're fumbling around for a light switch in the dark. You are the teacher, you are supposed to know how to find what you need, but you don't. At least I didn't. In the beginning, to help me teach, I was reading lessons from books, sometimes right out of my lap, but I didn't *understand* writing and writers' craft. Just know it takes time and you need to be patient with yourself. In my lessons section (Chapters 7 through 10), in each introduction to every lesson, I have tried to explain whatever craft or point is in the lesson, so that you will see what I see through the pacing lens. But there is one important thing to remember, you have an ace-in-the-hole: your students. I'll explain.

I know we want to understand what we have to teach. I know I can guide my students to see a lot more in writing now than when I first started. I also know that every year I see more craft in the same book, and my students discover new things I have never seen. I am always learning. Just remember, especially if you are just beginning to learn about reading like a writer or are not sure why or how a piece is crafted in a certain way, you have a room full of learners. Ask them. Their brains are in the habit of learning. They will figure it out for you. Don't worry, there is never any one "right" answer, only answers that make sense.

This works, really. If you'd like, practice nodding and looking like you know the answer and it's part of your very smart teaching plan to have them figure it out. That's what I did, and sometimes still do, although now that I know more about what I am teaching, I am quite comfortable with saying "I really don't understand how the writer paced this part so well, let's figure it out together." I am authentically modeling lifelong learning behavior. That's good, it's very good. In fact, it's probably the best teaching I will ever do.

Whether you pretend not to know or you really don't, having your students do the inquiry work is always beneficial. For example, for years I was nervous to teach poetry. I just didn't get it. Poetry. At all. I would actually get stomachaches for weeks before starting the unit I had promised only because the whole class was begging. Finally, I saw that I didn't have to "get it." It didn't matter what I didn't know or didn't understand, my students could do the inquiry work!

I remember them asking me, "Why does some poetry have ending punctuation marks and some doesn't?" (I had no clue.) "Great question!" I responded, "Let's divide into punctuation-in-poetry study groups and you can figure it out!" So we divided up and I passed out study stacks of poetry books and they began their inquiry and I anxiously waited for their results. When we came back together on the carpet, I charted what they noticed. (At least I can be the recorder.) I don't remember it all, but I do remember a couple of writer-in-the-making students who were getting really good at this point in the year at reading like writers. One student said there were periods in this poem because of the sad content, the writer needed you to come to a full stop at the end of every line, it brought a heaviness to the piece. The other said there were no periods at the end of the lines in this other poem because the writer wanted you to *linger* (she tilted her head back and waved one arm gracefully into the air) at the end of every line. I nodded thoughtfully. Heaviness. Linger. Works for me.

Since then I realized I can use free verse poems to support studying craft, content, and conventions in small pacing work. I educated myself by reading all of Georgia Heard's books, particularly *Awakening the Heart* (1999). I attended two of Georgia's Saturday workshops and I sat in the front row, hoping that would help. It did. I have gotten a lot better with poetry, even writing some of my own. My students help me.

Working Both Sides of the Coin

When thinking about guided inquiry, there is one more point to mention here. Writing instruction should not stay in the writing time of the day. Remember the other side of the coin. It's the reading connection that you need to make solid in your students' brains, to create that habit of mind. Back up your writing time work by asking students, in their independent reading time, to watch for and put sticky notes on pages where the author uses a specific small pacing or big pacing craft technique that you are studying. You and they will find that different writers, across different genres and for different reading levels, will be using the same techniques. (See Chapter 4 for one bit of small pacing craft in particular, a great one for scaffolding this plan.) With specific inquiry steps that you will be leading (see the chapters that present lessons), and lots of practice, your students will be able to find specific small pacing and big pacing craft on their own. They will develop the habit of mind of reading like writers, in your writing workshop, in your reading workshop, and in their independent reading time. Reinforcing the connection between writing and reading is a powerful way to keep those coin sides flipping, spinning until they become one.

Students on Their Own

Eventually, one by one, your students will internalize the habit of mind of reading like a writer. They will leave your structured learning nest and go off on their own. They will start bringing you things they notice in their independent reading, different craft than what you've been studying, probably things you've never seen, or at least never noticed. Great! You'll say. Now, where can you try that in your own writing? Students know exactly where. That's probably why they noticed it. They try out the new move in their own writing. It works. Then you'll know the reading connection is working. This is a fundamental skill that can be taken to any curricular area, by the way. Noticing, asking questions, labeling, envisioning, and applying. You are creating a lifelong learner in any field of endeavor they chose.

Zach

One year my student Zach was the first to go off on his own, finding a craft example that he liked in his independent reading and using it in his own writing. We celebrated by sharing his find and his application with the class.

He found a bit of well-crafted internal monologue in Matt Christopher's *Skateboard Renegade* (2000), page 84, in the ninth chapter:

> And he was, too. He was sorry about everything: sorry he'd bleached and spiked his hair, sorry he'd taken his sister's money, sorry he'd lost her earring, sorry he'd stolen the other one, sorry he'd ruined his jeans, sorry he'd gone to Amherst—sorry he'd ever been born!

Zach said it reminded him of the "what-if" strategy that we had just studied. (See Advanced Small Pacing Lessons, Chapter 10.) He labeled it the "Sorry List." I admired his find and asked him if he planned to use it in his own writing. He already knew where; he was working on a narrative about when he set a towel on fire while roasting marshmallows. He sat down to write what you see in Figure 3–1.

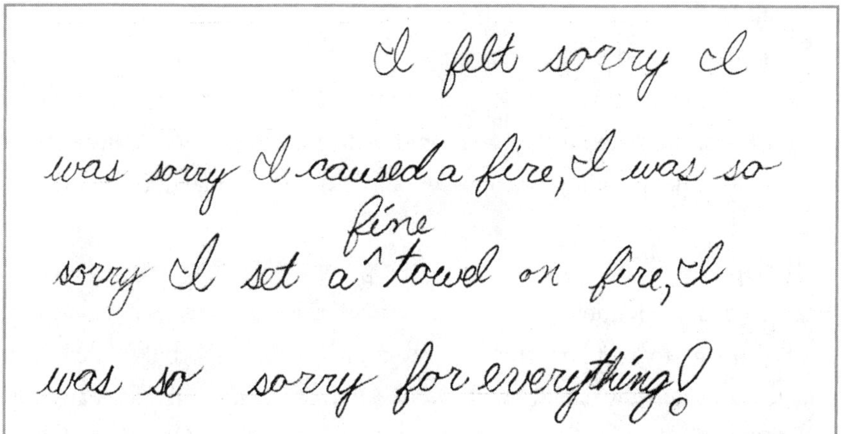

FIG. 3.1 *I felt sorry. I was sorry I caused a fire, I was so sorry I set a fine towel on fire, I was so sorry for everything.*

Sometimes, often times, our student writers will not see exactly how to imitate the structure of a craft move. The new learning is filtered through everything they already know and have internalized. They need help noticing, really seeing, the structure of something new to them. So Zach and I had a close look at the construction of Christopher's Sorry List in a conference and he made modifications to his own Sorry List (see Figure 3–2):

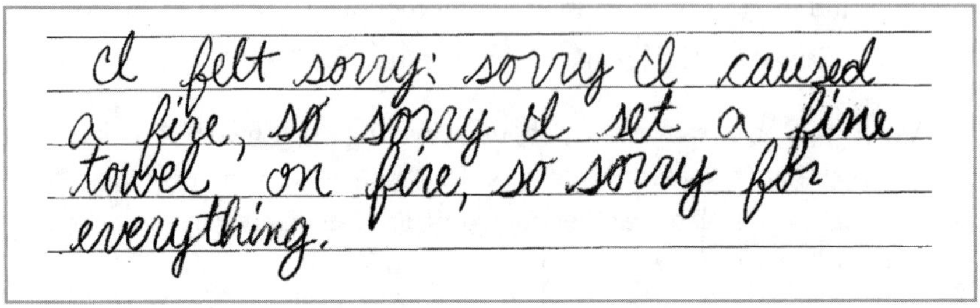
I felt sorry: sorry I caused a fire, so sorry I set a fine towel on fire, so sorry for everything.

FIG. 3.2 *I felt sorry: sorry I caused a fire, so sorry I set a fine towel on fire, so sorry for everything.*

If you are teaching students the inquiry process so they can learn to read like writers and apply what they've seen to their own writing, then it's just a matter of time before they go out on their own, finding and using all sorts of interesting craft moves, like Zach did.

Aakash

Most students need explicit guided instruction in the inquiry process. But some students have that "ear" and will do it on their own. And if you are reading a lot of well-crafted text and reading really well, then those students will pick up the skill of reading like a writer before you even fully understand how to teach it.

When I was first learning to teach writing using the writing process and the writing workshop model, I didn't know much about how to teach it, but at least I knew enough to say to my students, "Use a mentor text!" I couldn't tell them how to use one really well, but somehow some of them got the idea anyway. One of my students, Aakash, chose Cynthia Rylant's *When I Was Young in the Mountains* (1993) for his mentor text. He said he wanted to write his memoir about his dad "like this book." He was a quiet student, and an English language learner, who struggled in some areas. But I remember that moment clearly when he choose Rylant's book from our basket of genre mentors and hugged it tightly. He had made up his mind. He had a clear vision for his piece and he got to work.

I know I did not teach what Aakash shows in his piece—the elements from Rylant's book that he imitated—the long sentence structure (not typical for third-grade writing) that slows the pace, the rhythm of the repetition that sets up each vignette that is the organizational structure of the big pacing, and the reflection that ties it all together at the end. I didn't teach any of it because I

I remember the time me and my dad jogged together in the cold freezing morning to the tennis court with our tennis balls and our Rackets.

I remember the time me and my dad went out in the snow and I followed his big foot steps.

I remember the time me and my dad went to Buger King for the first time and when we sat down he smiled at me.

I rememer the time when me and my dad made lunch together and he taught me how to make my favorite food. I said, "thanks dad." He said, "No problem."

(Continues)

FIG. 3.3

Super Dad
by Aakash

I remember the time me and my dad jogged together in the cold, freezing morning to the tennis court with our tennis balls and our rackets.

I remember the time me and my dad went out in the snow and I followed his big foot steps.

I remember the time me and my dad went to Burger King for the first time and when we sat down he smiled at me.

I remember the time when me and my dad made lunch together and he taught me how to make my favorite food. I said, "Thanks dad." He said, "No problem."

I remember the time that my dad was really mad. I was afraid to ask him to watch the Winter Olympics with me. So I bravely asked him. He said yes. So we sat down on soft cool couch. I slowly got the T.V. control from the tabletop. I turned on the power and we watched together.

I remember the time when me and my dad went after dinner in the cold and freezing and windy and cool night air.

I remember when me and my dad went to the theater and we saw the movie "Lost Ships" we thought was so interesting.

I remember the time that my dad was really mad. I was uns afriad to ask him to watch the Winter Olympics with me. So I bravely asked him. He said Yes. So we sat down on soft cool couch. I slowly got the T.V. Control from the table top.

I turned on the power button and we watched together,

I remember the time when me and my dad went after dinner in the cold and freezing and windy and cool night air.

I remember when me and my dad went to the theater and we saw the movie "Lost Ships" we thought was so interesting.

(Continues)

FIG. 3.3 (continued)

All these times with my dad are very special to me. Whenever I need him he is there for me.

FIG. 3.3 (continued)

didn't understand it. Well, I must have at least pointed out the repeating line, it's so obvious. What I did, I remember, is read the book to the class, many times, as well as I could. Aakash mentored himself to the sound of Rylant's writing. He picked up the flow, the balance, the rhythm of writing directly from what he heard. And through this reading connection, Aakash produced his moving piece.

I do remember the editing conference I had with Aakash about his memoir. I remember telling him that "me and my dad" was grammatically incorrect. But at least I was smart enough to let him keep it as it was. We reread his piece out loud with "my dad and I" and it just didn't have the same meaning. Changing that convention would have changed the craft of it and the content, and his voice. It wouldn't *sound* right. It wouldn't sound like a child who loves his dad. I told him what I was thinking, and that I was also trying to think, have I seen this particular deliberate incorrect grammar usage anywhere else? Yes, I had. When my son was young, he had a book by Mercer Mayer titled *Just Me and My Dad*. The grammar had bugged me then, too. But for Aakash and his piece, I did not insist on a grammatically correct change, leaving the final decision to him. He kept "me and my dad" and I saw I was letting go of the sterile, grammar-right days of my English "writing" classes. I was learning.

Jackie

A few years later I was doing a better job of leading my students down the reading-like-a-writer path. Take a look at the end of Jackie's memoir, "In Mississippi" (Figure 3–4).

I recognized the purpose of the small pacing craft in this "show not tell" scene. The implied sadness of the simple short and then very long sentence

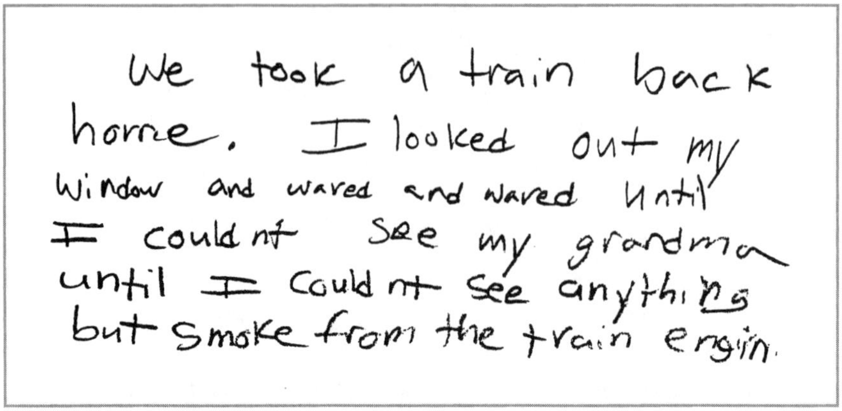
We took a train back home. I looked out my window and waved and waved until I could nt see my grandma until I could nt see anything but smoke from the train engin.

FIG. 3.4 *We took a train back home. I looked out my window and waved and waved until I couldn't see my grandma until I couldn't see anything but smoke from the train engine.*

that has no commas so you are short of breath. Perfect for the content. I knew I didn't exactly teach this literary way of writing. So I asked her about it, expecting her to identify a mentor text that we could share with the class. "That's beautifully written. Were did you get the idea to craft it that way?" She shrugged and smiled and said "I dunno." I knew all the scaffolding I had done to strengthen the reading connection was working in subtle ways now for Jackie. And we shared *her* writing with the class.

English Learners and the Reading Connection

The reading connection is so powerful that I have noticed it working very well for my English learners. It's interesting. They learn to write better than they can speak whether they have reading fluency in their primary language or not they learn to write with craft in their English writing, even if they have difficulty reading English fluently or even more trouble speaking it. I will see those problems with subject-verb agreement, or plurals, or verb tense, or articles, depending on what their primary language is. But I will see craft in their writing, because I am explicitly teaching them to read like a writer.

Haruka speaks, reads, and writes Japanese at home and at school. (See Figure 3–5.) Haruka learned to use what we called the "what-if" strategy (see Chapter 10). She used it as a revision strategy because, she told me, the pace of

It was a cold winter day. I was in
my car looking out the window.
I was thinking about skiing.
What if I can't ski? What if I
get hurt? What if every one laughs at
me?

FIG. 3.5 *It was a cold winter day. I was in my car looking out the window. I was thinking about skiing. What if I can't ski? What if I get hurt? What if everyone laughs at me?*

—*Haruka, from her "Mount Rose" memoir*

the beginning of her story was too fast without it and she wanted to slow it down with a thoughtshot (Lane 1993), meaning internal monologue.

And if they don't have reading fluency in their primary language, they still learn to write better than they speak. Ricardo, in his narrative about swimming (Figure 3–6), wrote very well.

Sowe I drid and drid and
dird then I nodest that I
was swimming.

FIG. 3.6 *So I tried and tried and tried then I noticed that I was swimming.*

Ricardo speaks Spanish at home and, that year, to his friend in class. This sentence sounds literary. He not only shows craft in the repetition of "I tried" as well as the use of sentence length, but he also is using, correctly, the complicated past participle verb tense. These are things I explicitly taught—more accurately, guided my students to learn—in our work of reading like writers.

I have heard it said that many writers write well intuitively, like a painter who produces a beautiful canvas without conscious thought of the steps he or she may take. I don't really believe it. I am sure that an intuitive writer is very well read and that the painter knows master painters' works. And if they thought about their craft, they could identify which parts are like other artists' works, which parts are their own synthesis (influenced by other artists), and which parts are there for what purpose. Creating art is difficult. Great artists in any medium work hard developing their skill and learn from those that come before them and those that surround them.

The thing is, we're teaching kids, with all their different learning abilities and all their different levels of competence in English. We have high standards to reach, or at least aim for, and have a short amount of time to meet them. We don't have time to wait for them to grow up, reading all the while, then intuitively become good writers or even *writers*. That's why we must use the reading connection explicitly to our, and their, advantage.

Then again, sometimes being explicit will fall on deaf ears and silent pencils.

A Reluctant Writer Is Rescued by Reading

I used to think there was no such thing as a reluctant writer. You know, those students who absolutely, no matter what you do, refuse to write. I was convinced passion and explicit teaching is all a teacher needs to transform every student into a writer. My passion led the way in my writing workshop. Everybody wrote, by golly, every day and they were excited about it. Until Jack. Jack was not excited. He wouldn't get excited. No matter what I did. He was bright, but he had his own agenda, which was reading, reading, and reading. You know the child. They read while walking down a hall, during a math test, while you're lecturing—tucking their book just out of your notice, they think, under the lip of their desk. You can walk right up to them and clear your throat, but they won't notice you, they're gone into the pages.

Jack logged 176 chapter books that year. The only time he had no book in hand was during writing minilessons. He would try to read, but I insisted, and since he couldn't hide it from me in the open in our meeting area on the carpet, he complied. He would sit with the group on the carpet and look vaguely at me for a brief moment, then gently poke a child next to him, or fiddle with his shoelaces, or roll himself under a desk. I was never sure how much, if anything, he was getting of any lesson.

When it was independent writing time, I would take his book out of his hands and hold it saying, "Good writers read, Jack, but they also write." He would take out yellow draft paper and shuffle it around, sighing heavily. The moment I turned my attention to another student he would pull another book out of his desk. When I stayed next to him to insist he write, he would mope and hang his head, rolling his pencil back and forth across the empty paper. Eventually he completed a personal narrative that went something like this:

> I went on a field trip in first grade. I went on a school bus. I saw lots of animals at the zoo. We saw (long list of all the animals). It was a fun day.

Then it was back to his book. During the year, I continued to do everything but cartwheels to try to get Jack excited about writing. All of my teaching, of course, for Jack and for everyone, was tied back to our mentor texts. We can improve our writing by learning to read like writers! I would exclaim, constantly. What do you notice in this text? I would lead, constantly. Yes! I can hear the craft moves of our mentor writers in your writing and it sounds great! I would confirm, constantly. Was Jack being at all influenced by the growth going on all around him? Was he listening? Was he getting it?

I saw he began to tune in when we did a literary nonfiction study. He loved octopus. And he loved that it was okay to read and read about them, out in the open while researching for his informational piece. For the introduction to his piece, he mentored himself to Jean Craighead George's *Look to the North, A Wolf Pup Diary* (1998) and he wrote a beautiful beginning (see Figure 3–7).

I had evidence he was learning to read like a writer. He had one piece of writing for his portfolio that he was happy with. Now, if those 176 narrative books would just come through for him.

Finally, toward the end of the year, Jack decided he would revise his zoo trip piece. He worked on it for just two writing workshop times, about an hour and a half, altogether (see Figure 3–8).

All that reading came through for him. This was a 176 book success. He still complained that writing was "very, very hard and gives me a headache" but he complained with a smile. He was very proud of this piece. He knew it sounded good. He had somehow internalized the complexities of purposefully control-ling the pacing in his writing. From the slow buildup on the bus—to the intense whirlpool of frantic separation—to the slide into a satisfying resolution. Perhaps he got a bit after all from all the lessons and inquiries I directed, I'll never really know. But I believe it's more likely that his writing was rescued by his abundant reading.

One more remarkable thing about Jack—his first language is Chinese. He goes to Chinese school in the afternoons, every day, and he speaks Chinese at home.

I love octopuses, they lured me to many aquariums to study them, they have never disappointed me.

Why do I love them so?

I like their style when they swim with their tentacles trailing behind them in the water as if they're dancing on the ocean floor.

I like their amazingly soft body which gives them super flexibility when they need to squeeze through a tiny crack to make a home or avoid enemies.

I also like them because they are smart. They can even change colors to blend themselves in with the surroundings.

I can go on and on about why I love them, but It's time for you to learn all about octo-puses. . . .

INRODUCTION

I love octopuses, they lured me to many Aquariums TO study them, and they have never disponited me.
why do I love them so?

I like Their style when they swim with their tentacles trailing behind them in the water as if they're dancing on the ocean floor.

I like their amazingly soft body which gives them super flexibility when they need to squeeze through a tiny crack to make a home or to avoid enemies.

I also like them because they are smart. They can even change colors to blend themselves in with the surroundings.

I can go on and on about why I love them, but It's time for you to Learn all about octopuses....

FIG. 3.7

It will be a rare child (and language learner) who will read 176 books in one school year, absorb pacing strategies and show them in their writing. For everyone else, we explicitly facilitate learning. We point out and share what is happening in what we read. Then we have students purposefully try out strategies in their own writing.

This story is about when I was still a 1st grader, I went on a fantastic field trip to the Oakland Zoo. Here is my story.

It was Tuesday morning. I was in Mrs. Chau's class, room 4. We were waiting for more of my classmates and the adults who are the leaders of each group of kids.

When it was time, We lined up. We walked to the bus. There were two bases, So we went in the second bus because the first one was fall.

It was a long, bumpy ride. There were other classes, so it was a little noisy, too. After the long, bumpy, noisy ride, we were finally there, at the zoo.

We got out of the bus, letting fresh air meet our noses. We lined up, and walked there. We had to wait in a line to get in the zoo. Some kids were playing on the rails. I joined them. By the time I stopped,

(Continues)

This story is about when I was still a 1st grader, I went on a fantastic field trip to the Oakland Zoo. Here is my story.

It was Tuesday morning. I was in Mrs. Chau's class, room 4. We were waiting for more of my classmates and the adults who are the leaders of each group of kids.

When it was time, we lined up. We walked to the bus. There were two buses, so we went in the second bus because the first one was full.

It was a long bumpy ride. There were other classes, so it was a little noisy, too. After the long, bumpy, noisy ride, we were finally there, at the zoo.

We got out of the bus, letting fresh air meet our noses. We lined up and walked there. We had to wait in line to get in the zoo. Some kids were playing on the rails. I joined them. By the time I stopped,

FIG. 3.8

I noticed my class was gone and I was lost.

I rushed in and was looking around and around, panicking. Crowds of people were rushing past me. It felt like people were swirling around me, as if I was caught in a whirlpool. Then my mind suddenly went blank. I didn't know what I did but I know I did something.

Finally, the Vice Principal, Ms. Armstrong, found me. She took me to where my class was waiting for me. My classmates said, "Jack, where were you?" My classmates looked relieved. Then we started our day at the zoo and I was careful to not be lost again.

> I noticed my class was gone and I was lost.
> I rushed in and was looking around and around, panicking. Crowds of people were rushing past me. It felt like people were swirling around me, as if I was caught in a whirlpool. Then my mind saddenly went blank. I didn't know what I did but I know I did something.
> Finally, the Vice principal, Ms. Armstong, found me. She took me to where the class way waiting for me. My classmates said, "Jack, where were you?". My classmates looked relieved. Then we started our day in the zoo and I was careful to not to be lost agian.

FIG. 3.8 (continued)

What About the Standards?

Are we taking all this time doing all this reading like writers work because we've come to understand it's good teaching? Yes. And the folks writing standards know this. It's in my district's standards, in my initiative's standards and you will find reading like a writer articulated in the NCEE New Standards.

In the fourth and fifth grade reading standards (E1b):

■ evaluates writing strategies and elements of the author's craft.

From the third grade writing standards regarding style and syntax:

■ Students meeting third grade standards when they leave third grade have a strong sense of "sentence sense." They use more "writerly writing," modeling and responding to the increasingly complex kinds of reading they are doing. Their style and syntax show an awareness of the choices a writer makes to produce a particular effect (for example, suspense) or to produce a certain kind of reading (getting the expression correct). Their writing reads like many of the books they hear in class, and they often embed borrowings, such as refrains or phrasings, from familiar books.

When we teach writing, we are really facilitating learning for our students by exposing them to the influence of good literature. If we do our jobs successfully, we will create a room full of students who can read like writers, identify craft that appeals to them and, most importantly, try out that craft in their own writing. It's the reading connection. The spinning coin.

Before we go to teaching pacing (lessons are provided in Part Two), let's have some fun gaining a deeper understanding of it. There is still much to explore in mentor texts around pacing. Gaining a deeper understanding can only help us teach the concepts at a deeper level.

We'll start with one phenomenon that occurs in writers' craft in big and small pacing strategies, so frequently across so many genres that it deserves a chapter all its own: the phenomenon of three.

4

The Phenomenon of Three

Language is the most perfect work of art in the world.

—HENRY DAVID THOREAU

I have heard it said that learning to read like writers, something that we end up doing as good teachers of writing, ruins our personal off-hours, reading-for-pleasure time. We bring this new perspective to our reading, noticing the *way* our favorite novelist crafts his or her book. I have heard it said it can be irritating to sink into a story, or any piece of writing, only to be pulled out onto the page when you can't help but notice a particular way with words. I disagree. When I admire a painting, I step back to enjoy the whole, to have a sense of what the painting is telling me, but I also step close to admire individual brush strokes; they're what deliver the message I believe being in the story or on the page is all part of the same experience. Why not enjoy the whole thing?

As you step in and look closely at writing you will frequently find in the brushstrokes a phenomenon of things occurring in sets of three. Arranging things in sets of three is one of the many small pacing craft strategies a writer has to create rhythm, flow, and balance in his or her writing. You can lead your students to this phenomenon with guided inquiry (see Advanced Small Pacing—The Magic Three, Chapter 10) and you will notice, as they begin to apply sets of three to move the flow of their own writing, that their writing will become more literary sounding, more artful. You and your students will find sets of three across all genres, done in big and small ways. Here are a few examples:

But I must get him close, close, close, he thought.
—Hemingway, *The Old Man and The Sea* (1987)

We bumped along, along, along the winding lane.
—Sharon Creech, *Fishing in the Air* (2000)

During the rest of antiquity the Acropolis and its magnificent temple were honored, admired and maintained.
—Lynn Curlee, *Parthenon* (2004)

We were so busy hugging and eating and breathing together.
—Cynthia Rylant, *The Relatives Came* (1993)

These are texts where the writing is stunning, rereadable, read-aloudable.
—Katie Wood Ray, *Wondrous Words* (1999)

A book is like a man—clever and dull, brave and cowardly, beautiful and ugly.
—John Steinbeck, making a comment to his editor, Pascal Covici

The essence of the way zealots think about the world is polar: good and evil, holy and profane, them and us.
—Anna Quindlen, *Newsweek*, "The Last Word, Life of the Closed Mind" (2005)

So Henry walked and walked, and he called and called, and he looked and looked for his dog Mudge.
—Cynthia Rylant, *Henry and Mudge, The First Book* (1987)

You could revise any of these quotes, but when you take out the threes, you take out the rhythm, the art:

Henry walked a long time while he called and looked for his dog Mudge.

Sets of threes are found outside of literature:

A magazine ad for sunglasses: Style. Substance. Seregeti.

The tag line on my home workout tape: Decide. Commit. Succeed.

From Winchester College, England: Either Learn, or Leave, or Be Beaten.

I would hope this last one is definitely outside of literature. I found it referenced in Edgar Schuster's *Breaking the Rules* (2003). Schuster includes it in his first chapter where he traces the stern beginnings of grammar. It is centuries old. And we can go even further back in time to find Julius Caesar's Veni, Vidi, Vici. (I came, I saw, I conquered.)

My students have identified and labeled a set of threes they call the short, short, long. Or maybe I gave them that label because I read it in *Wondrous Words* (Ray 1999, 177). I don't accurately remember. Wherever the name came from, notice, the first "short" is typically the shortest, in number of words or phonemes:

We looked. . . . We listened. . . . We decided to take the shortcut home.
—Donald Crews, *Shortcut* (1992)

She didn't eat, she didn't sleep, and my silly brother forgot what spot of
earth held the seed.
—Sherry Garland, *The Lotus Seed* (1993)

But that's okay, because the history of a kid is one part fact, two parts
legend, and three parts snowball.
—Jerry Spinelli, *Maniac Magee* (1999)

Short, short, longs are in the commercial world too:

A magazine title: Sierra: Explore, Enjoy, and Protect the Planet
A birthday card from my dentist: Here's hoping your day is fun, festive
and filled with smiles!
An ad for a movie: THE WILL TO SURVIVE. THE STRENGTH TO
ENDURE. THE COURAGE TO FACE THE TRUTH.

I can't help noticing threes everywhere now. Just when I think I might be taking a little mental break from thinking about writing, relaxing at the hairdresser, waiting my turn, looking over the selection of magazines, I see there between *People* and *Cosmopolitan*, on the cover of *Business Week*, June 27, 2005 a short, short, long:

Old. Smart. Productive.

Turns out, this short, short, long is the beginning of the fourth paragraph in the cover story by Peter Coy. Three one-word fragments. Together they make a powerful rhythm that brings a forcefulness to the writer's point about the vitality in the graying of the workforce. It wouldn't work the same written any other way.

In *Miz Berlin Walks* (1997), Jane Yolen crafts a list of story topics, three of them, at the end of a long, complex, single sentence. Notice how she arranges them shortest to longest:

> But if she said: "Well, child, I remember once upon a time . . . " she'd tell a real whopper of a tale, about clever Jack, or that bad girl with a mouthful of toads, or the ghost that walked each night under the whispering trees.

Would the small pacing work as well if we rearranged the order? There are six possible ways to order a set of three. Let's try a few:

> She'd tell a real whopper of a tale, about that bad girl with a mouthful of toads, or the ghost that walked each night under the whispering trees, or clever Jack.

Maybe. But it is not as smooth. It brings the rhythm to a stop with the shortest at the end. It leaves you expecting more about Clever Jack. In Yolen's story, there is nothing more about Clever Jack. How about:

> She'd tell a real whopper of a tale, about the ghost that walked each night under the whispering trees, or clever Jack, or that bad girl with a mouthful of toads.

Feels bumpy. Your breathing just isn't quite right for the story's overall soft and flowing content unless you read it the way Yolen arranged it: shortest to longest. Jane Yolen is masterful with the rhythm in the pacing of her writing. But why is it that so many writers, masterful or not, in literature and advertising, use the short, short, long thing? And are they doing it purposefully or intuitively? I can't say for sure. I would imagine as writers they check their work, reading it outloud to themselves, and when they hear that it doesn't "sound right" for their purpose they revise it until it does sound right. It's back to the reading connection—the reason to always be reading quality literature to your students, so they can internalize what "sounds right" in our written language, which will help them to hear what sounds right in their own writing.

My students and I have seen short, long, short or an occasional long, short, short combination in writing. But these have a more final sound to them, not the rhythm that occurs with a short, short, long that works to smoothly continue the pace.

Longer Threes

The following examples are still sets of three, but now a bit longer; the threes are separate sentences. Here is an example of a set of three questions that begin the second paragraph in Seymour Simon's *Wolves* (1993):

> But what is this animal of our imagination truly like? Are wolves savage and destructive hunters of people and livestock? Or are they one of nature's most misunderstood creatures?

A set of three sentences (also a short, short, long) end the fifth paragraph in Chapter 2 of Jerry Spinelli's *Maniac Magee*:

> Some say he just got tired of running. Some say it was the butterscotch Krimpets. And some say he only intended to pause here but that he stayed because he was so happy to make a friend.

My son has been after me to read Lemony Snicket's *Series of Unfortunate Events*. They're funny! he promises. I am not so sure. Every time I pick up one of Snicket's books and begin to read I find a dire tale. Recently, trapped in the car on a long drive with my son, he seized the opportunity and began to read Snicket aloud. Lucky for me. He was just starting Book the Ninth, *The Carnivorous Carnival* (2003). It's opening is loaded with threes:

> When my workday is over, and I have closed my notebook, hidden my pen, and sawed holes in my rented canoe so that it cannot be found, I often like to spend the evening in conversation with my few surviving friends. Sometimes we discuss literature. Sometimes we discuss the people who are trying to destroy us, and if there is any hope of escaping from them. And sometimes we discuss frightening and troublesome animals that might be nearby, and this topic always leads to much disagreement over which part of a frightening and troublesome animal is the most

frightening and troublesome. Some say it is the teeth of the beast, because teeth are used for eating children, and often their parents, and gnawing their bones. Some say the claws of the beast, because claws are used for ripping things to shreds. And some say the hair of the beast, because hair can make allergic people sneeze.

Next there's a paragraph where Snicket takes a little break from the threes, followed by this paragraph:

> I am sorry to tell you that this book will use the expression "the belly of the beast" three times before it is over, not counting all of the times I have already used "the belly of the beast" in order to warn you of all the times "the belly of the beast" will appear. Three times over in the course of this story, characters will be inside some terrible place with little chance of escaping safely, and for that reason I would put this book down and escape safely yourself, because this woeful story is so very dark and wretched and damp that the experience of reading it will make you feel as if you are in the belly of the beast, and that time doesn't count either.

I count seven sets of three, some intertwined, in these two paragraphs. Fun, but a little too thick for my liking. I feel like the pacing is bogged down, tangled up, with only the threes to give it some small sense of control. Then I remembered that a writer's choice of pacing supports their content. Bogged down, tangled up, with some small sense of control is perfect pacing for this story which, in the next paragraph, presents the Baudelaire orphan characters (the three of them) bumping along a dirt road, hiding inside the trunk of their nemesis' car, planning what to do next.

Threes in Big Pacing

Snicket also takes us to my next point about the threes. A set of three can help to organize big pacing. In his beginning of Book the Ninth, Snicket announces the organization of his plot to his reader. He tells his reader to expect the characters to be in "the belly of the beast" three times over the course of the story. I did not finish reading this dire tale to find out if that is indeed what happens. My son assures me it is.

I find sets of three in the big pacing in many of my favorite picture books:

In *My Rotten Redheaded Older Brother* (1998), author Patricia Polacco crafts three main scenes where she is trying to beat her brother at something—berry picking, rhubarb eating, and merry-go-round riding.

In *White Water* (2001), authors Jonathon and Aaron London create three scenes of riding a raft through rapids, each one a little scarier and a little longer than the last.

In *The Worry Stone* (1996), author Marianna Dengler organizes three stories within one.

Storytelling is filled with threes: three tasks, three wishes, three times huffing and puffing in *The Three Little Pigs*.

A Writer's Choice

Cynthia Rylant's *Henry and Mudge: The First Book* is loaded, loaded, loaded with threes. So is her *The Relatives Came*. Why is that? In the coming school year I plan to ask a small group of students to do a "Cynthia Rylant and the Search for Threes Study." I am curious to find out, is it just her style? Will we find them in all her books? If we do, does that mean all her books have a similar, lyrical pace that is a natural fit for so many threes? In the meantime, I have noticed that some authors use a lot of threes, some use an occasional, and some use not one.

A Lot of Threes

In *Going North* (2004), author Janice N. Harrington uses a recurring set of threes: the sounds of the tires on their station wagon, taking the family away from the South to the North:

listening to the tires make a road-drum, a road-beat: good luck good luck good luck

(You need to get this wonderful book to notice how the white space and font are used.) Another example:

Mississippi on and on, Mississippi, Mississippi going by.

But then the content of the story changes, and the craft of the pacing changes with it. The threes change to twos:

Gas gauge getting low, getting low.

And on the next page:

Will this place serve Negroes? Gas gauge says almost gone almost gone.

The family finally gets gas and we slide back into threes in the "road-drum" of the tires, and in other threes sprinkled throughout and to the end.

An Occasional Three

In *Thundercake* (1990), Patricia Polacco did not use many threes. I found just three, altogether. Here are two in a row:

The air was hot, heavy and damp. A loud clap of thunder shook the house, rattled the windows and made me grab her close.

A lot of threes would not have the right rhythm and flow to support the content of this story of a jumpy and scared child working hard and getting over her fear of thunder.

Not One Three

I picked up Jean Craighead George's literary procedural book, *To Climb a Waterfall* (1995), expecting to find at least one three. I remembered from a previous read-through that I had been impressed with the overall pacing; the beautiful word choice keeps you moving step by step along a peaceful unhurried hike up to a waterfall.

When I took a closer look at George's small pacing craft, I noticed she did the entire book in twos. Not one three. Why? When I thought about, I decided twos make more sense for the feel of a hike, for the pacing that takes the reader through the entire book: right foot left foot, step by step. Remember, especially when you are considering the "why" of writers' craft, there are no "right answers," only ones that make sense to you and your students. She writes:

the home of the waterthrush and the otter.

Grab their roots and pull yourself up.

The climb becomes steeper, the water wilder.

You are there. Stand up.

She did all this and many more twos. Her book would not read with the same step-by-step rhythm and flow if she used threes instead:

the home of the waterthrush, the otter and salamander.

Grab their roots, hang on tightly and pull yourself up.

The climb becomes steeper, slippery, the water wilder.

You are there. You did it. Stand up.

If we asked her, could Jean Craighead George articulate decisions she made about her pacing? It would be fun to find out. But no matter, we have a special task as teachers. It is our job to lead our students' journey into the world of literature. It is our job to explore "the most perfect work of art" with our students, the whole thing, the painting and the brushstrokes. So they can learn. And we can learn, too.

Part of exploring literature to help us understand writing and help our students learn to write well is to see the role that the rules of grammar play. Let's go there next.

The *Ands* and *Buts* of It

To teach writing well you need to have an intellectually open mind. Writing is an art form, wonderful and surprising, large and complex, open and inviting. To bring to your writing instruction a small, orderly package of handed-down rules: never start a sentence with *and* or *but,* no fragments, no run-ons, and so on, is to bring to your writing instruction a closed mind. How can a teacher serve students well, stiffly carrying such a small package, when the whole, wide writing world is full of *ands, buts,* fragments, and run-ons, and anything else a writer needs to use to make his or her meaning clear?

The more I learn about writing, the more I don't understand how the package of rules continues to exist in our writing world. There is a plethora of award-winning writing to show the contrary. And then there is the truly amazing thing about some of the "rules"—they aren't rules at all. They are mythrules (Schuster 2003) with a life of their own. Mythrules with no identifiable origin.

Let's consider this mythrule: never start a sentence with *and* or *but.* One can simply infer this is indeed a mythrule by noticing the number of sentences beginning with *and* or *but* in fine writing everywhere. I appreciate Janet Angelillo's (*A Fresh Approach to Teaching Punctuation*, 2002) long hours spent with a colleague in New York City Libraries hunting for the written origin of this mythrule. They found nothing. It simply doesn't exist.

We also have the factrules (Schuster 2003), which you can trace to some printed source. Either way, myth or fact, they give us a small package to teach from. Either way, the package exists because teachers choose to deliver it. We *choose* to deliver it. Is there hope?

I have a sense that many of us are beginning to unwrap this package and have a closer look. I believe this is happening because as we take the time to actually study real writing, we see it is not possible to craft a beautifully paced, breathing piece of writing with stiff, dead, prepackaged rules.

So, is this okay? Or, is there one type of writing that *writers* can do and another type of writing that students should do? Let's think about other curricular areas for a moment. We would certainly not be doing our students any favors in math or science if we were to establish a school curriculum that does not match what they will see and need to understand to succeed outside of school. We wouldn't say, "Yes, well, that's how *real* scientists and mathematicians conduct their thinking, but in school, we're going to do things *this* way."

I would like to think that we are teaching math as it is expected to be done, outside of schools, in the math world. And we are teaching scientific process as it is expected to done, outside of schools, in the science world. And we are teaching writing, as it is expected to be done, outside of schools, in the writing world.

Yet, this is not always the case. I hear the English Teacher Grammar-Draconian alive in so many of us. She's like J. K. Rowling's Voldemort, weakened by the powers of the good and the truth, but powerful enough to continue finding ways to live on. I hear her speak (wielding a ready red pen) when someone in an audience of elementary school teachers questions the "correctness" of an obviously purposeful, indeed beautifully crafted sentence fragment that the presenter has shared with us. "Should we be teaching our students to write like that?" she asks. Or when a friend's child, in middle school, tells me that her English teacher told her to never start a sentence with *and* or *but*. I explained to her that sentences can and do start with *and* or *but*. This child took my statement back to her teacher who retorted with, "Yes, but that kind of writing is not considered *good* writing." Okay, then, someone had better announce that writing by countless folks like Charles Dickens, E. B. White, Hemingway, and other modern award-winning writers for children and adults including Pulitzer Prize winners like Richard Russo and Edward P. Jones, and any others you'd like to randomly pull off a book shelf, is not considered *good* writing

Since we plan to use actual, good quality writing to teach our students how to write well, then we had better start to study it. If you teach from the package—the mythrules and factrules—in the morning during your word study, then you open a book in the afternoon to study what *writers* actually do, you had better be ready to eat your grammar. I give my students one rule: You may write anyway you would like to write, as long as your writing reads like you know what you are doing. That about covers it. I don't say you can break the rules as long as you know the rules because they are young and I don't want them to have to deal with that sort of conflict. (I can just see the breaking the rules idea taken to a recess game.) And if you think about it, so many of "the rules" aren't rules at all, so why go there?

Our students learn the art of using language in writing every day as we read and study well-crafted, well-paced writing. They are learning what sounding like "you know what you are doing" means. I cannot teach them to become attuned to the sound of good writing with a rules-of-grammar package. The package, isolated from real-world writing, is stiff and flat; it does not breathe.

Grammar in Context

It's a matter of how we think about our writing instruction. It's a matter of our approach. We can teach the rules, alone and in isolation, or we can integrate. What will best serve your students? Consider unwrapping the package and integrating grammar rules into your reading like a writer instruction. Consider constructivist learning theory. Your students will make the most sense out of grammar rules, traditional and nontraditional, when taught in the context of real-world writing.

I do teach conventions. I do appreciate grammar, punctuation, and correct spelling for the tools of communication that they are. I try to teach as much as possible in context, around grammar as craft in the writing we are studying. Around punctuation marks as the meaning conveyors that they are. I even do some grammar worksheet work (as similar as I can get to what they might see on a state achievement test). Mostly, I am always identifying parts of speech when teaching the whole class or in a small-group or an individual conference. That's how to talk about writing. There are words available and I use them. *Verb.* I do not use *action word* since *action word* doesn't always make sense to students. The action is not in the verb in the sentence, "They had a fighting chance." *Adjectives, adverbs, prepositions, nouns, pronouns, conjunctions, subject, predicate, clauses* and *phrases,* and so on. I use the actual names of parts of speech. I integrate. We look at grammar in context so that we can see how these parts of speech work together. I name them so there is a common language to talk about craft, to talk about pacing, to talk about writing. A student might say, "I don't like the way it sounds here, it's not smooth." And I might ask, "You mean the way your prepositional phrase in the beginning here makes the sentence sound bumpy?" Over time, if we are all talking this way, our students will acquire names to label what they already have a sense about and are learning more about every day: language and when it sounds right.

When one of my students, Claire, crafted a powerful lead to her memoir (see Figure 5–1):

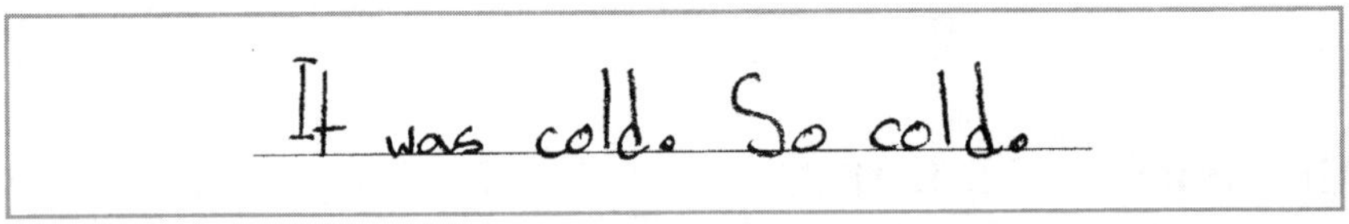

FIG. 5. 1 *It was cold. So cold.*

I said, "Bravo, Claire! You have a simple, short sentence followed by a purposeful sentence fragment and you have them in a paragraph all to themselves. With just these five words, you have really emphasized to your reader just how cold it was." She nodded and nodded because she already understood about short sentences and fragments and short paragraphs and how writers use them for emphasis. She knew she had a fragment because there was no subject. She knew the fragment could work because the subject was implied. We had noticed such writing in our mentor texts. I gave my students the grammatical labels, we studied the writing, and we asked why. Claire was learning grammar in context. In the context of what she read and what she wrote. In the context of craft. Her writing reads like she knows what she is doing.

We do need to know about grammar to craft writing well. And there is a lot to know. To check my grammar, to make sure I have my dependent and independent clauses correctly identified, I am always referring to *Grammatically Correct* (1997) by Anne Stilman. (Another must have!) She says things like—this is the typical usage here, but a writer can make a stylistic choice and do it this other way. I like that. It shows a thinking connection from the rules to writing in the writing world. I also refer to *The Chicago Manual of Style, 15th Edition* (2003) and of course, Strunk and White's *The Elements of Style* (2000). These resources remind me of the words and factrules and terms that I should be using to talk about writing. I would like to be correct when I grammatically label and teach what is going on in grammar, in sentence structure. But I don't expect the sentence structure to always be following the rules. (Did you notice my split infinitive? *to be always following the rules* just doesn't have the rhythm I want.)

Cleaning House

Every now and then I go through the clutter that seems to collect around my house, gathering dust. I sit down and have a careful look at this or that item before I decide to pack it off to Goodwill or the landfill. Do I need it for anything? Is it useless but I cannot part with it because of a sentimental attachment? Then I make the decision to either get rid of it or carefully wrap it up and stow it away where it takes up room in my garage. Maybe the next time I look at it I'll have the courage to part with it. When I am through, and I look around, I feel better. I can't think surrounded by clutter.

Let's take some time here and do some clutter cleaning. Let's have a careful look at that package of handed-down rules. If we don't throw them out now, or at least store them in the "garage," they will be a problem in learning to understand and teach pacing well, as you'll see. As teachers, to best prepare our students for the writing world, instead of preaching from the package, we must look closely at what writers do. Look *closely* at what writers *actually* do. We've done a lot of that already, let's keep going, package in hand.

I am not writing a book on grammar. So I am going to tackle just a few examples to make my point. If you are telling your students never to start a sentence with *and* or *but*, and other such mythrules then please stay with me here.

Learning from Writers

Whenever I begin a study with my students looking at craft uses for pacing with the word *and*, invariably someone will pipe up with "Never start a sentence with *and*." It seems to be such an all-powerful rule that students don't even feel the need to raise their hand for permission to speak it. It comes out on its own, sitting largely in our classroom like the elephant that it is. I am always ready.

"Who told you that?"

"My mom."

"Mmm, yes. I have heard that before."

I pause. The student stares. All students stare, waiting, they've heard the same thing. The elephant shifts its weight, sensing its imminent demise. "Your mom is wrong." (Gasps and giggles all around.) "But it is not her fault. Somewhere, sometime, somebody who doesn't understand what writing can be told her that. Remember, we are learning about writing from *writers*, so let's have a look at what *writers* do."

Then I whip out *Fishing Sunday* (1996) by Tony Johnston and show them the two-word sentence on the very first page, "And still." A fragment to boot. I've read this book to them already, but it's likely at that point in the year they were just enjoying it as readers, not studying it as writers, or if we had started reading it like writers, we were not focused on the *ands* and *buts* of it yet. Next we launch into the first of many, many discussions that we'll have throughout the year about rules, mythrules, knowing the rules and when writing sounds good while not following the rules. I'll often read the story of the battle that took place about sixty years ago between a magazine writer and his editor. It's on the first page of the chapter titled "Hyphenation" in Stilman's *Grammatically Correct* (1997). You've got to get a copy and read it, my summary below will not do it justice:

> *The writer did not want a hyphen where the rules said he should have one. The editor did. The writer stuck by his intent and the editor stuck by his grammar until around 2 a.m., when the editor got tired and the writer won.*

I share this story with my students because it opens their young minds to a larger, historical world of grammar and conventions and rules and the possibility for discussion and individual choices around writing. Individual choices. And changing one's mind about what the rules are.

I continue the conversation with my students: "Tonight you can teach your mom something about writing that she doesn't know." (Big smiles that show the awesome power that is our community of learners.) "If you'd like to take a handout home, I'll have one available later today with examples for you to use in your discussion with your mom."

With the mythrule elephant now out of the classroom, we continue with our inquiry work, seeing how authors actually use *and* in crafting their small pacing. Later that day, I will be sure to have the handout available to support the fact that never start a sentence with the word *and* or *but* is indeed a mythrule.

My handout consists of examples of *ands* and *buts* in plain use from authors and books, newspapers and magazines that my students' parents might recognize. I've included them here for you if you'd like to make up your own handout using these examples. Or, you may have fun finding your own examples. They're everywhere. (I have included pacing commentary here that I don't include in my parent handout.)

From the Narrative Genre

In Charles Dickens' *Great Expectations*, there's not just a sentence, but a paragraph that begins with *and*. There are many other examples in his book that you could use, of course, but this just happened to be the one that was sitting there waiting for me on the very first page I randomly flipped to. It's the fifth paragraph in Chapter 3.

> And yet this man was dressed in coarse grey too, and had a great iron on his leg, and was lame, and hoarse, and cold, and was everything that the other man was; except that he had not the same face, and had a flat, broad-brimmed, low-crowned felt hat on.

This is also a beautifully crafted, factrule-breaking use of a conjunction with a series comma, with the comma and the *and* placed together to create an intense rhythm to the small pacing of this character description by pausing at and emphasizing each consecutive detail. This craft move supports the content, by *showing* the reader the narrator's shock at the appearance of the man instead of *telling* it in some grammatically correct way.

In E. B. White's *Charlotte's Web*, there are heaps of examples, but I noticed a lovely set of three in a row at the end of the first paragraph of Chapter 3:

> And whenever the cat was given a fish-head to eat, the barn would smell of fish. But mostly it smelled of hay, for there was always hay in the great

loft up overhead. And there was always hay being pitched down to the cows and the horses and the sheep.

What is the small pacing purpose here of these *ands* and a *but*? You need to look at the paragraph in its entirety. What I see is that these three sentences melodically close a paragraph that begins with short sentences and then gradually builds into longer ones. The *ands* emphasize that there is so much that brings serenity to this peaceful barn. They add to the mood, they soften your breathing. Read the sentences without the *ands* and see what I mean. (Remember, too, that E. B. White is coauthor of the quintessential Strunk and White's *Elements of Style*. Just a point to ponder. . . .)

How about an example from a Pulitzer Prize–winning author? How about Ernest Hemingway? He apparently found that starting sentences with *but* was essential to telling his tale, *The Old Man and the Sea*. There are so, so many. I'll share a few, starting with the third sentence of his beginning:

> But after forty days without a fish the boy's parents had told him that the old man was *salao*, which is the worst form of unlucky, and the boy had gone at their orders in another boat which caught three good fish the first week.

Hemingway could have divided this sentence into two sentences at the comma, starting the second sentence with *and*. But he chose, for a softer rhythm for the lead to his story, to have a run-on instead. Read it the way it was written and then read it as if it were two sentences. The flow is changed and the meaning is changed, ever so slightly.

There are three examples in this paragraph:

> But, he thought, I keep them with precision. Only I have no luck anymore. But who knows? Maybe today. Every day is a new day. It is better to be lucky. But I would rather be exact. Then when luck comes you are ready.

And many, many more. What is the craft purpose here? I don't pretend to know how to analyze Hemingway. And as the sentences starting with *but* occur throughout, I think we'd have to have a look across the entire story. I did, and it seems to me, in pacing a story of such conflict, the frequent use of the word *but* to start so many sentences brings a back-and-forth swing appropriate to the pacing of this tale of struggle. This small pacing strategy directly supports the content. Used throughout, it supports the narrative in a big pacing way.

There are plenty of examples of starting sentences with *and* or *but* and other myth- and factrule-breaking writing in modern Pulitzer Prize winners as well. I invite you to pick up any writing by your favorite adult or children's authors and take a close look.

Outside of the Narrative Genre

Perhaps, if you are a package holder, I have begun to convince you that teaching from the rules may not best serve your students. But perhaps you are also thinking, Well, okay, that's narrative writing, I'm willing to give these writers a bit of poetic license, but certainly I would not teach my students to write a feature article or an essay without strict adherence to the rules.

I understand. We have a responsibility to serve our students well. So let's leave the bookshelves; let's leave narrative and have a look at other genres of writing. However, *I* am sticking by *my* point: We are preparing students to communicate ideas through well-crafted writing, narrative *or* expository, as it exists in the real world. When you begin to look, to read like a writer, you'll notice rule-breaking everywhere. Let's look at a couple of examples.

While sitting in my dentist's waiting room looking at *Newsweek*, I flipped to Anna Quindlen's "The Last Word." In her seven-paragraph article, "Life of the Closed Mind," she uses *but* to start four sentences. Her very last sentence starts with *and*.

For my students' parents, I photocopy Quindlen's entire article onto the backside of my handout. I circle the *buts* and the *and*. You can probably find it archived on the Internet. But I hope you are seeing my larger point. Pick up *anything* by a writer that people generally respect, in any genre. You'll find *writers* do not follow mythrules and they purposefully and artfully break factrules.

My local newspaper, *The San Jose Mercury News*, had an article that a colleague shared with me. Because of the content, not the craft. It was reporting the success of a foster child who was moved from home to home his whole life, but ended up finally graduating from Stanford (de S'a 2005). My colleague thought one of my students at the time, also a foster child, might enjoy the article. He did. So did I. And I couldn't help noticing, and being delighted with, the craft that de S'a used to pace her story so the reader would get it. Emotionally.

This is her entire fifth paragraph:

> Before launching his PowerPoint presentation, Madrid asked the audience to get up, gather all their belongings, and move. Once seated, he asked them sternly to please do it again. And again. And again.

She could have written it with factrules and mythrules in mind: "Then Madrid continued to sternly ask his audience to move." But the craft of the small pacing would be lost and so would the force of the point, the emotional impact, and therefore, the meaning. Notice she left those "And again" fragments hanging, alone, at the end of the paragraph. This repetition is most powerful this way, as it should be, to support the content: Madrid's continually uprooted childhood.

Are you going to keep looking? Perhaps in the *New York Times*? They're in there, broken rules. Perhaps a highly scored state writing test essay? They're in there, too. I refer you again to Ed Schuster's book (2003), *Breaking the Rules: Liberating Writers Through Innovative Grammar Instruction.* In the example that he includes of a highly scored state writing test essay, that was later ripped apart by teachers for errors, the student writer appears to understand the only rule that really matters (as did the people scoring her essay): If your writing reads like you know what you are doing, you can do anything in your writing.

Writing is an art form to convey meaning. Writers know this. Let's follow their lead.

Leap of Faith

My mother is a retired high school English teacher. I remember when I was very small looking at stacks of student papers she would correct evenings and on weekends. They were covered with red ink.

As I got older, I noticed her stacks changed, she traded the red pen for a pencil. Red was too harsh, she told me, I want my students to improve. I am still marking errors, but I am also writing positive comments and helpful notes. I learned people change their ways, trying to improve themselves and how they help others.

Recently, my mom has begun to teach again, tutoring English to individual students whose parents are a nervous wreck over the addition of the writing portion of the SAT. As I was writing this chapter, I wanted feedback from someone who carries the package of rules, who thinks of teaching writing not by studying great writing, but from expecting adherence to the rules.

I knew my mother carried the package. It's how she learned, it's what she taught, it's what she knows. I wanted to hear the voice, the reaction to this chapter from someone who first reads writing for errors. Without telling her my intention, I emailed my chapter to her. She called me back, excited, "Do you have it in front of you?" It was late, I was half asleep, "Go ahead, mom, I have it memorized."

She plowed into my errors:

- I should replace *which* with *thus.*
- I should not leave "from" at the end of a sentence.
- I repeated one word too many times in one paragraph.
- I missed several subject/verb agreements (I corrected those).
- I used *their* instead of *his or her* (I corrected that).
- I should change *like* for *as* (Mmm, *like, as, as, like,* okay, I changed it, but I will not call it a correction; it's a choice.)

I was smiling. Here was the voice of a teacher with the package. The errors are addressed first. I decided to push a little. As we were nearing the end of page 2 I interrupted her, "Thanks mom, could you please read the whole thing for content and call me back?" She did. Her tone had changed. She was pleased.

Once she got into it, she said, she liked the rhythm.
She liked the detail of the personal anecdotes.
She liked my word choice.
She liked my sense of humor.
She liked my variety and control of long paragraphs and short ones.
She liked how I made a strong point then pulled back to let the reader
    "chew on it." (She liked my pacing.)

She was still critiquing the writing, but she was one step back from the errors, looking now at more of the overall writing. But I was still dying to know what she thought of my direct attack on teaching writing from just the rules. I interrupted again, "Thanks, mom, what do you think about what I have to *say*?"

Her tone changed again, she was thoughtful.

"I like what you have to say." (She hadn't read any other part of the book.) "I think you are saying we expect these writers as having fine writing, yet we don't teach to their writing and we should."

Then she thought out loud about what she had read about what the scorers were expecting from a good SAT essay: clear, smooth (well-paced), and well-made points, and there would not be a big emphasis on looking for errors, for the package. Here is one source:

Kaplan, *The New SAT 2005 Edition*
Chapter 3: SAT Writing Basics, page 22:
The essays will most likely be scored quickly and holistically by two readers. Holistically means your essay gets a single score—a number —that indicates its overall quality. The number takes into account a variety of essay characteristics including organization of information and ideas, sentence structure, vocabulary, and grammar and usage. Thus, a highly persuasive and eloquent essay that has several run-ons or other minor errors could still mean a top score because of its overall effectiveness and impact.

Then she said, "I have the responsibility to continue to learn if I am going to teach." I quickly scribbled down such an enlightened statement. And finally, "I am going to change the way I teach."

I felt privileged to be a witness to her synthesis. My mom is one example of a teacher willing to be thoughtful, reflective, and make the leap from that restrictive package of rules to learning about writing from writers. She understands the value, for ourselves and our students, of being open and flexible in our thinking, of being a lifelong learner.

I told her to run out and get Schuster's book before she leans on my one little chapter. As well as Ehrenworth and Vinton's (2005) book, *The Power of Grammar.* I must add here, after our conversation, I sent my mom the rest of Part One of this book, as it was almost completed. She has since been calling me occasionally very excited about the amazing results she is getting by showing her students how to read like writers, the dramatic improvement in their writing, and how much they're enjoying writing now. Those are really quick results. Almost makes you want to move up a few grade levels.

For Those Who May Not Have Leaped

A caveat: There is one consideration I ask my students to always be aware of. Their audience. They need to always ask, Who are they writing for? In the future, students may indeed be writing for a teacher who still carries the package. The teacher who has announced the *and* and *but* rule as a fact. And who knows what else. Will she give a low grade on a paper if they break the rules? Will she care to listen to them explain and support their knowledge with examples? I tell my students they will need to decide what to do when and if that time comes. But since I think (I hope) I am noticing the gradual disappearance of this particular *and* and *but* elephant that hopefully further enlightenment will follow. I am optimistic that fairly soon no student who has learned to read like a writer will ever be confronted with such an uncalled-for dilemma of having to decide between serving a teacher's needs and all the possibilities that are found in good writing.

In my classroom my students learn this is one standing rule: If your writing reads like you know what you are doing, you can do anything in your writing.

Now with this business out of the way, we can proceed to teach our students to learn from *writers.*

Postscript

A student brought this example to me during his independent reading time, sometime after we had done a punctuation study:

> Every few seconds, small drops of moisture would fall from the fungus
> with a *plop!* and the children had to duck to avoid getting light tan fungus juice on them. Like the small crabs, the *plop!*ing fungus did not appear to be very harmful, . . . (Snicket 2000, 34, emphasis author's)

I had never seen anything like that before, the use of the second exclamation point. I've seen and used the first. I know what to say to a student when they bring me interesting craft, and I started to say it, "Great! You are reading like a writer!" But I didn't go on like I usually do and ask where he was planning on trying this interesting use of punctuation in his own writing. I was too shocked. The exclamation point was doing its obviously intended job—when I read it out loud it really did sound like that fungus was plopping. But I couldn't get past the fact that I had never seen an exclamation point in the *middle of a word.* My student waited and watched while I struggled. He probably read my face as I was thinking, Jeez! You really can do *anything* as a writer. I wish I hadn't shown my doubt. He likely had an idea of where to try it in his own writing. It never showed up.

Reflecting on this incident now tells me I still have a way to go. The package never made it to the landfill or my garage. It is apparently clinging to the bottom of my shoe.

Teaching Pacing

The lessons I have here for you to try and tweak are explicit. They are filled with examples next to nonexamples to help our student writers understand pacing. They are filled with suggestions for guided inquiry using mentor texts. I have included many student work examples to help you see what I have seen in my students' work. I have included a few examples of lessons where I use my own writing. I hope you will write with your students and use your own examples as well.

I typically have more than one way to teach each lesson. You choose. Sometimes, with a particularly difficult concept, I have taught the same lesson a new way each day for a few days in a row. I know if I just keep opening different doors to the same concept, my students will eventually get it. Some meanings just take longer to construct then others.

At the beginning of each lesson, under Previous Lessons/Background Knowledge Needed, you can see where the lesson falls in a set and also what work you might want to cover in your word work or grammar skills block of time before the lesson. At the end of each lesson, you will find reading workshop support and homework support—for extended practice and reinforcement— that I have found are essential toward helping to build meaning and eventual internalization of pacing strategies.

These are obviously not all my lessons from one school year. And I am continually adding and changing lessons according to my students' needs along with growth in my understanding. These are lesson sets to get you started, to see possibilities for everything-is-tied-to-pacing teaching. It's a thinking curriculum. Think about what I have presented here, then think about what would work best for you and your students.

You will need high expectations. We can ask so much of our students because each of them is capable of more than we can imagine. Don't set the ceiling, open the door.

Above all, these lessons will work best with your sense of excitement and awe for the process and the product. Writing is an art form, as much as music and painting is art. Passion is essential to appreciating, creating, and sharing art.

A Note on Charts

I have included only a few examples of charts from my classroom. I keep binders of photos of every one of my charts; they help me with next year's planning so I remember what worked and what didn't. But they are charts that I created with my students. You and your students will work up your own. I have given you ideas of what might go on a chart; you'll find those in the occasional bulleted list. These lists are not "the" chart, they are to help you understand what you are looking for before you guide the inquiry.

I do make some charts ahead of some lessons, my charts for direct teaching lessons, for instance. I am not asking what they notice in a text we are studying, I am telling them what I want them to learn, so why waste their writing time by having them watch me write up the chart?

Guided Inquiry Versus Direct Teaching

Most of the lessons are done in some varying sort of guided inquiry way. I do plenty of short, direct, minilessons throughout the year, especially on days when I just need to make a quick point and students are anxious to work on their writing. But generally, the more difficult the concept is to teach, the more I lean on guided inquiry. Over the years I have learned I get far better results from guided inquiry into difficult concepts than from teaching the same lesson in a direct-teaching way. I see the results in the writing of both my English only students and my language learners. Guided inquiry gives them the chance to figure out concepts and construct meaning each in their individual ways.

I do more guided inquiry at the beginning of the year while students are building stamina for long blocks of independent writing time and while I am helping them build the habit of mind of reading like a writer. Later in the year, I will do more lessons in the guided inquiry format toward the beginning of a unit as we are following the steps of inquiry to learn the genre, or the focus of our unit. Then I will taper off guided inquiry to more direct-teaching mini-lessons around specifics I see they need from ongoing assessment of their writing projects.

You can easily change every lesson I have for you into a direct teaching lesson. Just read it through, see the point to teach, and explain the point—the craft move and the purpose—to your students. You may want to do that now and then, when time is an issue, or if direct teaching is the way your workshop usually runs and you'd like to step into guided inquiry one toe at a time.

Please know the guided inquiry work is usually directed toward such a specific outcome, that leading a guided inquiry won't take much longer than a direct lesson, especially as you do more guided inquiry work, and you and your students get better at it. The biggest bonus in taking the guided inquiry path is eventually you will have a room full of students who are always teaching themselves, because they have learned to read like writers.

How Part 2 Is Organized

You will need to start with Chapter 6, Presenting Pacing to Your Students, to set the groundwork. Then go to Chapters 7, 8, 9, and 10 for the lessons.

Know that the lessons are *not* grade-level specific. They are skills specific. You may disagree with me on whether a lesson should be considered basic, advanced, or used in a revision unit, as part of a set or by itself. That's fine. Teaching writing is fluid. A thinking curriculum. Observe, think, and decide what you should teach next based on your students' needs. I have the lessons loosely arranged in order. But you decide what lessons to use and what order works for you and your students and which of your own lessons you will insert and add.

A Little at a Time

As you are deciding which lessons to use and in what order, please consider this: Don't teach all these lessons plus your own all in one long unit of study. It won't work. I remember first starting out with an eight-week-long narrative picture book study. It was too much for my students to try to learn all in one unit.

I take the standards a few at a time, two from the genre standards and two from the language use and convention standards. Those standards guide me in my choice of lessons and lesson strings. We focus on those standard elements in a two- or three-week study, then we publish and celebrate. Students write reflective letters. I assess their writing and plan the next unit. I tell them I expect to see them applying what we learned in the last unit and but there will be more ways to improve their writing in this next unit. Slowly, but always through the pacing lens to connect it all, we build their writing skills from one unit of study to the next. With quick units of study, students get more practice with standard elements, and more opportunities to write better and better pieces.

On Choosing Mentor Texts

In any lesson, from any chapter, you will need wonderful writing to teach from—your mentor texts. I have found my favorites over the years and they have become my touchstones. You'll see them in every lesson, but some are currently out of print. Your city library may have them. Or you might find them used on the Net like I have; lovely copies discarded from various libraries and usually at reasonable prices. But you don't need the same books that I use. Use the books that you love. If you love them, they're written well, and if they're written well, they're paced well. Have a new look at them. Give yourself some time. Maybe get together with your grade-level team and study them for pacing in the craft, content, and conventions. Using your understanding of pacing gained from Part One of this book, you will be able to locate examples for all my teaching points. If you have trouble seeing the pacing, remember you can have your students to do the inquiry work, too.

If you don't have piles of books to choose from or even a few favorites then I suggest you visit your local library. I recently stood patiently behind a woman returning 224 picture books to our city library. I didn't ask if she ever paid late or lost fees. But I would think borrowing books until you and your students discover favorites to learn from is a better idea then just buying randomly recommended books that you may not end up loving. I have a bunch of those.

On Revision

I do revision units. I tell my students part of a writer's process is to put away a completed piece of writing, work on other pieces, and then months later take out the put-away work and have a fresh look at it. I tell them Stephen King (2000) writes about how he does this in his memoir. He waits months to do revision work to a completed first draft. I tell them Stephen King has a formula: second draft equals first draft minus 10 percent. I tell them because they are beginning writers, their formula might be finished piece plus 10 percent. Or more.

Just to be clear: I never tell them we will be revising their memoirs in a few months when they are in the throes of trying to finish them. I might have a mutiny on my hands. They finish their pieces, we celebrate, we move on to other genre and units of study. Then months later, I tell them the Stephen King revising plan and they are excited to have a look at writing they did months ago. I think they are also excited, at that point in the year, to do a quick unit of study with something they don't have to start from scratch.

I know how they feel. Personally, I prefer revising over drafting. At least with revising, I've got something to work with.

I know I also need fresh eyes to assess my students' work. After a few months have passed without looking at their pieces, I can more clearly see things like: pieces a bit thin here and there, gaps in the flow, missing segues or transitions between a fast-paced part and a slower part, underdeveloped detail, causing the reader to have questions or to wish to linger longer in a particular part. In other words, I can more clearly see the incomplete pacing. After studying their writing and seeing what they need, I choose lessons that will help them take their finished memoirs and make them better.

I have found this plan—doing a revision unit on a piece that they have already finished—works well. Most of the writing is done already. They enjoy hearing the Stephen King example of what *writers* do, and they tackle needed changes with interest and fresh energy.

On Using Your Own Writing (Or, a Word to the Frustrated)

How much of a writer do you have to be to teach writing?

While trying to figure out what good writing is, what well-paced writing is, you have to look closely look at how writing is done by *writers.* It's a little scary, getting so close. Especially when you are told to teach writing well you should be writing, keep a writers' notebook, just like your students, (I do, and they see me write in it and I share from it) include your own writing in your lessons, (I use the same drafts and finished pieces year after year) and model writing right on the spot (I typically work something up ahead of time). If you are not used to writing this way it can be frustrating, even frightening. How can we possibly write like the really good *writers* that we study? We can't. Well, maybe a few of us can, but those folks tend to peel off and become professional writers, like Eion Colfer did. For all the rest of us: First, it doesn't matter, we're teaching kids, we just have to get an understanding and a minor level of competence, we're not swinging in the major leagues. Second, and what does matter, is that you experience the process. It's the *process* that matters most. You need to be able to say with authority, Yes, I know how you feel, when I got stuck choosing a topic to write about I did this. . . . And, Yes, I know how you feel, when I got stuck trying to write a slowly paced description for the beginning of my memoir about my grandmother I looked at Jane Yolen's writing for help. Let's look together.

We are attempting to teach writing well. The writing process model makes more sense to us than any other way we know or were ever exposed to. But if we're going to teach it, we need to know it, just like we know and can do the work in all our other curricular areas.

How much of a writer do you have to be to teach writing? I would say not much. I am not a mathematician, yet I teach math. I am not a historian, yet I teach social studies, I am certainly not a scientist, yet I teach science.

We are teachers. That is so much. We know how to deliver material, how to help our students construct meaning for themselves. We can teach anything we are familiar with.

So write and become familiar with the writing process. Write a bit in the genres you teach. Learn the process for yourself and for your students. You will have experience to draw from, authority to teach from, and a certain comfort level that grows with time and practice. And nobody, including you, needs to be a *writer.*

Presenting Pacing to Students

S tudents need our help to construct meaning. They are just beginning their writing and reading lives. They don't see writing yet in all the complexities that we do. They need some concrete help, a foundation to build on. The foundation that I use for building the everything-in-writing-is-tied-to-pacing scaffold is a set of metaphors. I have a set because I am hoping to catch all my all students' different learning paths. I hope one of the following connections will work for you and your students.

Whichever one you choose, you might want to introduce the metaphor for pacing with something like this:

Pacing is a big thing. Pacing is what holds a whole piece of writing together. It will take us a long time to learn how to pace our writing. It will help if you think of it this way . . .

Writing as Art Metaphor

We know when music sounds good, when colors look right on a canvas, and when writing reads well. Good writing has a flow, a balance, a rhythm that our brains appreciate. Writing reads well when it's paced well.

This metaphor alludes to writing as an art form; it supports the idea of audience. It reminds you that you write for a reader, and readers have expectations..

A River Metaphor

Think of taking a raft down a river. Some writing will take you on a peaceful, journey, down a gentle, winding river. Some writing will take you on a trip over rapids. Or you could get a clever combination of both. But good writing will not leave you sitting stagnant, or lost and confused, or suddenly dump you off your raft.

My kids connect with this one. They love it, actually. It's a rare child who has been on a raft on a river, but they know what I mean because they have vivid schema of river rafting from movies, television, and books. To top it off, I have a favorite touchstone book, a mentor text I love and use repeatedly, Jonathan and Aaron London's *White Water* (2001), that they will have heard me read aloud many times before we get to learning pacing.

As we go through the year, I return to this river metaphor again and again to help students visualize and build their deepening understanding of pacing. For instance, if a piece of writing suddenly includes some meaningless or distracting scene, I might say that a gas station has suddenly appeared in the middle of the river. Or whatever, your students will make it up. If the story ending is too abrupt, we say the reader as been ejected from the raft, with no warning. If the writer has included too much and too many flowery adjectives, we say that a few pretty birds singing in the trees along the river are lovely, but an endless jabbering flock is too much. If there is no descriptive detail in the writing, we say the reader can't see where they are, they can't see the river or the river banks.

I even use the river metaphor to help students construct meaning for the importance of controlling grammar. I tell them things like: Loss of subject-verb agreement control or verb tense control is distracting; it's like thwacking your reader in the face with low-hanging branches that should be pruned (edited). I am even so bold (or sneaky) as to tell my students: Poor spelling gives your reader a bumpy river ride; how can a piece flow well if the reader is stuck trying to figure out your words? Suddenly the classroom dictionaries have a passionate use.

You can have a lot of fun with the river metaphor. There are endless possibilities for modifying it for students to help them construct meaning around any pacing point.

A Quilt Metaphor

You can think of pacing as a quilt. The big pacing is the whole thing—stand back and take a look at the overall pattern (content), how is it organized, can you see the balance in the patterning? Small pacing is in the patches—step close and take a look at the details attended to in just one of them (small pacing strategies to support content). Then look around the whole quilt, notice how the whole thing is held together by threads, some threads doing a straight and narrow job (conventions), some threads are artfully arranged into interesting patterns (craft). There are many different components, big and small, that come together into a pleasing work of art.

Of course students would need schema for quilts, which you could have a lot of fun providing.

Other Metaphor Ideas to Consider

Music

I tried to use a music metaphor once, but I think my students didn't have enough schema for complicated pieces of music with different layers—small and big pacing. They just stared at me blankly, then advised me to stick with the river metaphor. Maybe if I were teaching writing at a music school . . .

A Pacing Umbrella Chart

I have considered this one, but haven't tried it yet. The metaphor would be visual: A chart with a simple umbrella outline with big pacing as the umbrella cover and small pacing as the handle, and content, craft and conventions as the ribs. Over-simplified, I think.

A Venn Diagram

I have been trying to work up some sort of three-way Venn diagram, where each component—content, craft, and conventions—is in a circle. The part where they overlap is small pacing and the whole thing is on a larger circle or square or drawing of an open book called big pacing. But I am not happy with that either, although I like it better than the umbrella. The problem with visuals like these is that they limit students' thinking. The visuals take a concept that is so complex and multilayered and reduce it to an oversimplified state. Sort of like looking at a list of ingredients instead of enjoying the cake.

I do simplify my instruction as best I can, feeding students one little piece at a time. But I want them to first understand that what we're going for is complex and wonderful and there's no way around that. A printed list of ingredients might be interesting, but it's nothing like the cake. However, if printed ideas or charted ideas work for you, go for it. I prefer to use and modify the river metaphor, because I can see in students' faces and in their writing that it works best. Probably because I believe it and I can talk about it confidently. I use it in endlessly different ways with the whole class, or small groups, or in an individual conference. It is a concrete image on which the students can build an understanding of pacing, and the importance of their work as writers creating a fluent piece of writing for their reader to enjoy.

A Note About New Students

Because the classroom metaphor is so powerful as a scaffold, it's just what new students need. I get them on board with our classroom metaphor right away. It always surprises me how quickly new students learn about writing when submersed in the knowledge level of their class. I have found that missing bricks in their foundation can typically be filled in with a personal conference or two, or three, around teaching points from the basic lesson sets. By the end of the year, it's hard to tell the new students from the been-there-all-year students.

Basic Big Pacing Lessons

This chapter contains a set of basic big pacing lessons that I have taught for years with success. The lessons work together as more or less an ordered set, depending on what you see your students need. You may want to insert small pacing lessons into this series of big pacing lessons if your students need them.

For example, you might be teaching cutting irrelevant detail and building a bridge with time compression, but then notice that your students' small pacing skills are flat. All their sentences are the same length. So you decide, before teaching exploded moment (and they do a lot more flat writing), that you will stop the big pacing and go to small pacing. You introduce a series of lessons on sentence length and variety. Then you go back to big pacing, do the exploded moment lesson, and the students apply those small pacing strategies to help them craft their exploded moments well.

These basic big pacing lessons are a great place to start if you are new to teaching writing, or if your school is new to a writing process (workshop) curriculum, or if you have a group of students who are just beginning to develop as writers. Start here if your students have no sense of audience, no sense of what it is to create enjoyable-to-read, well-paced writing. Start here if your students' writing sounds like any of the following.

- Heaps of irrelevant detail. Nine pages written about the plane ride to a favorite relative with one paragraph for the relative. Or, more generally speaking, many pages of every boring "and then" detail of a day with maybe one paragraph, or section, or sentence about something potentially interesting and meaningful.

- "Bed to bed" personal narratives (Graves 1994). These read like just what they sound like: waking up, breakfast, teeth brushing, a list of every mediocre event of the day, followed by evening teeth brushing and back to bed.

■ Anything else you see that shows a complete lack of a sense of big pacing.

BASIC BIG PACING LESSONS LIST

1. Cut the Irrelevant
2. Building a Bridge with Time Compression
3. Explode the Moment
4. List Strategy
5. Purposeful Use of Dialogue

LESSON 1: CUT THE IRRELEVANT

Component: Content
Mentor Texts Used: *Owl Moon* (1987) by Jane Yolen, or your class favorite narrative picture book
Previous Lessons/Background Knowledge Needed: Students will need a first draft of a narrative to work with that shows at least a sense of beginning, middle, and end.

Lesson Introduction

In managing pacing, we are dealing with three pacing components: content, craft, and conventions. There is no point in tackling the craft and conventions of irrelevant content, so this lesson is a great place to start.

The first surefire way that a writer can ruin the pacing of their piece is by including irrelevant detail, irrelevant content. It upsets the balance, it upsets the flow, it upsets the rhythm. Have you read a novel where you are puzzled as to why the writer is spending pages and pages describing say, scenery in infinite detail? Why, you wonder, is the author wasting my time? I get it, and if I don't get it, I'll fill in the blanks as to exactly how much moss is growing on the rocks of the river bank so can we get back to the story, please. You, the reader, have been pushed out of the book by the writer's lack of control over content. The pacing is ruined. True in narrative writing, true in any genre. In fact, I have spent many, many a long hour combing through this manuscript seeing what I can chuck out. I don't want to lose you and I certainly don't want to waste your time.

Let's think more about the reading we do for ourselves. As adult readers, we have learned that every detail attended to in writing typically has a purpose. In narrative writing we expect details to move the plot or the action or to develop character. I learned quickly while reading

Dan Brown's *The DaVinci Code* (2003) that any little detail described or mentioned that might seem initially out of place or irrelevant, never was. That little detail was just a rolling pin, noisily left out on the counter so that later the writer could easily clack me over the head with it. I don't really mind a rolling pin story if most of the plot is fun, gripping, or otherwise enjoyable. But I do mind useless, unused, and otherwise annoying rolling pins.

Sometimes things aren't so obvious. Little details are gently, quietly slipped in and later the reader has the joy of finding the author's purpose revealed. Then the reader feels smart, literate, sharing a wink with the writer. Perhaps that growing moss on the riverbank is the subtle answer to the mystery of the lost heroine. But if it turns out that the all that moss has no apparent purpose whatsoever, then the pacing is lost in the irrelevant content. Reader annoyed. Pacing ruined.

We need to give our students this understanding. We need to explicitly teach our students that they should carefully attend to every detail in their writing, that every detail should have a purpose. Luckily, they are not writing novels with elaborate settings, complex plots, and deeply developed characters. They are writing relatively straightforward short stories, typically personal narratives. With some thought, they should be able to get a handle on their purpose, main idea, or focal point.

In my advanced big pacing lessons, I help students see and attend to story elements. I guide their thinking around the details in their writing with questions like, Do your details move the plot, develop character, give your reader a sense of time and place? But for this first basic lesson, I ask them to just focus on what they are really trying to say, the main idea. When they know what they are really trying to say, they can see in their pieces what is relevant and what is irrelevant. And with an understanding of main idea in place, the class can later move into advanced lessons around crafting story elements to support the main idea.

Fourth grade teacher, Susan Hull, has her students write the main idea of their personal narratives ("it was my first time on stage and I was scared") right on the top of their draft. Great idea! No irrelevant moss on rocks can get into that piece without being noticed! When the writer's purpose is clear, then the irrelevant stands out and can be crossed out.

Then there is the argument that writers often don't know what they are really writing about until they have had a chance to write a bit and discover their true purpose. In that light, asking your students to write their main idea across the top of their drafts is still a good idea. Just remember to give them the caveat that as they write they may find a different or hidden main idea; ask your students to keep in mind that writing can be a road to self-discovery so their stated main idea may change. You can tell stories of writers discovering the true meaning to their pieces long after they got started. For instance, a writer might comment: I thought I was writing about excitement of adding a baby brother to our family, but really I was writing about feeling that I had lost my dad to the son he had always wanted. Or, better yet, if you are writing with them, you will likely have such an authentic point to share and, bonus!, you can model your process.

In any case, asking students to think about their main idea, what they really want to say, will at least remind them that there should be a purpose to their pieces and they need to keep out the moss.

Using Your Own Writing

Even if you don't write a whole piece with your class, take some well-worth-your-while time and have fun writing just the beginning to a story and fill it with irrelevant detail. It is most effective to add irrelevant details like the ones you have been reading in your students' pieces. It brings the point home when they hear their own irrelevant bits of writing in your example. If it is early in the year and student writers are not quite willing to share their drafts with the entire class to get help from their classmates, then this ploy will work because you are not identifying students directly by using their actual pieces. One year I noticed students writing irrelevant things about their cats for some reason. And, as I notice every year in so many pieces, they were adding what exactly they were eating at various points in the story. (What is it with the food?)

My example looked like this:

> When I was young I lived with my family in an old house on the beach. I could step off the porch onto the sand that sloped down to the water's edge. Some-times, at night, the wind would carry sea foam to my bedroom window. I had a cat, too. Actually, we had three cats, but two were strays and we hardly ever saw them except when they were very hungry. So really we just had one cat. He was orange with white stripes. I really liked our cats. They were fun to play with.
>
> One day, I was left alone on the beach to watch my baby sister. She was sit-ting in the sand playing with some seashells. I was eating my snack. It was my fa-vorite kind of snack, peanut butter and crackers. Yum! When I wasn't looking, she stood up and wobbled down close to the water. She nearly drowned that awful day. This is what happened . . .

You get the idea. I added those last two sentences at the end so, for the purpose of classroom discussion, there would be no doubt as to the main idea of this incomplete story.

You can put your example on chart paper or on the overhead. In either case, get a pen and get ready to start crossing things out. Of course, be sure to empower your students; let them discuss and tell you what to cross out. You can use the river metaphor. Remind them they are working on a smooth river ride for their readers with nothing odd or out of place. When you're done crossing out, read it out loud as a group. Read your unedited version, then the crossed-out version. Ask them to notice, as you read, the difference in the flow. Then have them check for flow in their own writing by reading it quietly out loud, crossing out the irrelevant details. At closure, share struggles and successes.

Using a Mentor Text

Choose one of your class' favorite mentor texts and rewrite it "into the air" (that is, just talk out loud, instead of writing on a chart). Insert irrelevant detail similar to what you've seen in your students' writing. Do it dramatically. For instance, pick up *Owl Moon*, turn to the first page, and with a flourish, while looking at the page, read:

> It was late one winter night, long past my bedtime, and I was really excited to go owling with my Pa. But first I had to feed my dog, Scruffy. Then my mom said I had to brush my teeth before I went out. So I brushed my teeth. Then my mom made me put on my jacket and boots and scarf and mittens and hat. It took a long time to put on all those clothes! Finally, I went outside with Pa. [*Then continue reading the actual* Owl Moon.]

If your students know the story well, you will hear them groaning. Tell them writers purposefully control their writing for details. Irrelevant details will ruin their pacing. Ask them to consider, what is their story really about? What is their main idea? What details support their main idea? Ask them to cross out any and all irrelevant detail in their own pieces.

Looking at Student Writing

If your classroom is a safe writing community—and it should be for curriculum as personal as writing—be on the lookout for a piece of student writing you could use. Usually all but the very self-conscious writers are happy to have the entire class give full attention to their drafts on the overhead. They know they are benefiting from a massive response group—the benefit of all their classmates helping them with their work. And eventually, as the reticent see the safety and the rewards, they volunteer as well. In this focus lesson, the question to pose to your classroom of writers is, *What are they really trying to say? What is important and what is relevant to support that importance, to move and control the story?*

I have an example to share from the writing of a relatively strong student writer. Even the students who have moved way past writing bed to beds will still struggle with irrelevant detail in early drafts. I caught the problem in an individual conference. All I had to say was, "Whoops! Why is all this irrelevant detail in here"? I reminded the student, Henderson, to only include those details that would support his main idea. He immediately understood and wrote a second draft, right then. Lucky for me. I had his before-and-after drafts to share with a small group of new students, and here with you. Henderson is a language learner, Chinese, so you'll notice verb tense problems and apparently he had just discovered exclamation marks.

Figure 7–1 shows his first draft.

Henderson's piece sounded a little bit like *Owl Moon*, in one or two sentences, didn't it? It's called *close imitation* and it's okay. In fact, it's exciting. It happens when students study

It was one cold night when it happened. I already heard about that my cousins are going to come, one of them is a boy in college, the other is a girl who has a job, and drives a car. I was waitings for my cousins to arrive, there was no wind, and the street lamps outside were so bright, the street seemed to shine, until I saw it, it had to be my cousins who had arrived down from L.A. up to here! It felt like I had won the lottery! And ding dong! In they come! It was so exciting! And so, the next morning was officially known as, Christmas Eve, my cousins thought if they could take me and my brother out for Christmas shopping at the mall, my parents said, "Okay," and we were off, first the mall, then lunch at a restaurant and finally to the movies and home. My cousins had to go to a place I never knew, where they went. The next morning I went down to the T.V. room to open my presents, it was a cold Christmas day, I counted, 10 presents on the floor. Later that morning, my cousins took my brother and I out to the park's tennis court to play tennis.

FIG. 7.1

mentor texts closely; they begin to internalize the sounds of writer's craft. If a student ever crosses the line into plagiarism, I'll have a conference with the student and show him the fine line between novice writer imitation and copying.

Henderson revised his version, taking out the sound of *Owl Moon* and replacing it with the sound of this part of Jonathan and Aaron London's *White Water*:

Dad told me again how much fun white water rafting was. "And by the end," he said, "you'll learn to read the river—which way looks safer, which way is more dangerous."

I was quiet, thinking about how scary it would be. Here the river was flat, but what did it become around those huge rock walls?

Henderson's second draft appears as Figure 7–2.

I was pleased with Henderson's deliberate and thoughtful use of mentor texts to help him craft his writing and I told him so. We want our students to learn the sound of language by apprenticing themselves to favorite authors and then apply what they notice in their reading to their own writing. In this case, Henderson, by apprenticing himself to *White Water*, was able to improve the sound of his writing and find his main idea.

> One cold Christmas morning it happened, my cousins decided to take my brother and me to the tennis court.
>
> My cousin told me how much fun tennis was.
>
> "And in the end, you will learn how to play tennis."
>
> I was quiet, thinking about whether I can do it or not, fortunately, my cousins said that they would teach me, but how?

FIG. 7.2

Henderson is a third grader who is very bright and catches on quickly. But he is a young student writer, and as we saw in his first draft, he is still learning and does not have basic pacing strategies internalized like he will gain eventually, over time.

Reading Workshop Support

Facilitate discussions around main idea in your read-alouds and in students' independent reading. Use this reading connection to help students construct meaning.

Homework Support

Students need practice recognizing what irrelevant details look like and how they can bog down the pacing and don't support their main idea. Ask them to choose one of their previous writers' notebook entries that is narrative in genre, decide what the main idea is, then cross out all irrelevant details. Share successes and struggles the next day.

Related Readings

Craft Lessons, Ralph Fletcher (1998), page 82, "Pruning the Bushes—Cutting What You Don't Need," Grades 5–8

LESSON 2: BUILDING A BRIDGE WITH TIME COMPRESSION

Components: Content and Craft
Mentor Texts Used: *White Water* (2001) by Jonathan and Aaron London, *Beekeepers* (1998) by Linda Oatman High
Previous Lessons/Background Knowledge Needed: This lesson is meant to follow Big Pacing Lesson 1, Cut the Irrelevant.

Lesson Introduction

Now that students have successfully cut the irrelevant from their writing, they will be left with a lot less writing in their drafts. Sometimes many pages less. That's great!, you tell them. Now we can work with just what is important to tell your story. However, before you move on to Lesson 3: Explode the Moment to help them build up what is important in their narratives, you will likely have many students with what appear to be holes in their stories. The half page or more about a car ride to get a Christmas tree is now gone, but the student writer may wonder, how do I get my reader with me from my treeless house to the store and back? It's time to show them a handy pacing tool: time compression.

Remind your students that they are creating a smooth river ride for their reader, sometimes faster, sometimes slower, but always smooth. I draw a simple representation on the white board. I take a black marker to one end of my white board and start drawing a slightly wavy, horizontal line. Your reader, I tell them, is enjoying the pace of your story riding down the river you have constructed for them. Yesterday we saw that many of you all of a sudden dropped your reader into a hole (drawing an abrupt drop in the line, almost straight down) or in some cases a canyon (even bigger drop) of irrelevant detail. Your reader feels lost and confused down there (messy, squiggly lines) because you were writing about things that don't matter to your story, like brushing your teeth and what you had for breakfast. Then, you brought the reader back to your real story (bring the line back up and then continue the horizontal wavy line). Yesterday, you cut out all that irrelevant detail and brought the reader back up to the purpose of your story (erase the drop lines and squiggles leaving one long wavy line with a short piece missing in the middle). But there's a problem, you tell them. How do you get your reader from this side of the canyon to the other? Well, you could build a bridge for your reader (draw a line, you can even make it look like a bridge, that connects the two wavy lines). This bridge is called *time compression*.

Now you have a couple of choices:

1. Show them a few examples of time compression from your favorite books (prewritten on a chart) and send them off to write their own—direct teaching.
2. Show them one example from a favorite book and then have them look in study stacks to find more examples—guided inquiry.

I choose one or the other depending on time constraints. But typically I will choose the first choice, the direct minilesson approach as in, "here it is, now you do it." And then I spend additional time guiding students to discover time compression as readers in our reading workshop.

Using Mentor Texts

Linda Oatman High's *Beekeepers* has my favorite example of time compression so far. I love that it is in a set of three (refer back to Chapter 4) and that she reverses the order of the barn, pond, and trees for the character's return trip from the bee yard to the house.

> We walk across the grass, dew misting our boots, past the barn, the pond, the trees . . . and into the bee yard.

Make an example/nonexample chart. Write this lovely time compression on one side of the chart and on the other, write something irrelevant, wordy, and poorly paced like:

> After we got on all our beekeeper clothes we had to walk over to the bee yard. It took a long time because it was really far away from the house. We had to go past the big red barn with the old tractor inside of it. We had to go past the pond too. There were lots of ducks on the pond.

I could go on. You get the idea. The trick here to writing any nonexample is to make it sound like your students' writing. If your students are starting every sentence with *then*, write it that way. Whatever you see in their writing, imitate it. It drives your point home.

Point out that although Linda Oatman High wanted to get her characters to the bee yard, she knew not to distract her reader from the purpose of her story by ruining the pace of her story with irrelevant detail. She compressed their walk into one beautifully crafted sentence.

Be sure to show your students the sentence written in reverse later in the story when the characters return from the bee yard.

Looking at Student Writing

Many of my students take to the *Beekeepers*-style of time compression and use it in their writing. Figure 7–3 is Carmen's piece.

> Then later we walked past the roller
> coaster, snack shop and the soda machine to
> go see a show.

FIG. 7.3   *Then later we walked past the roller coaster, snack shop and the soda machine to go see a show.*

She could have just said, "Then we went to see a show" for her time compression, but mentoring herself to the sound of High's writing helped her write a fluent sentence. You can see Carmen's entire piece in Chapter 11, Language Learners and Reading Like a Writer.

Divyansh wrote what you see in Figure 7–4 about going to the store to get his first Christmas tree.

> We went past Braly school, past the
> four-way stop sigh and twisted and
> turned to the market.

FIG. 7.4   *We went past Braly school, past the four-way stop sign and twisted and turned to the market.*

He describes the hunt for the tree beautifully, but then see how he writes his time compression in this order for the trip back home from the store (see Figure 7–5).

> After we bought the Christmas tree
> and we put it in the car, we drove past
> the four-way stop sign, past Braly
> School and twisted and turned home.

FIG. 7.5   *After we bought the Christmas tree and we put it in the car, we drove past the four-way stop sign, past Braly school and twisted and turned home.*

I love the way he did not completely reverse the order for the trip back home. His small pacing rhythm is best with "twisted and turned" at the end of each sentence. And these two time compressions are far enough apart in his piece that you don't question the order, you just enjoy the sound of the writing. Notice how I have time compression here in these big pacing lessons because we use it to help control the organizational flow of the piece, yet we end up talking about small pacing? The small supports the big.

It is likely, in your conferring during their work on cutting the irrelevant, that you found some students struggling to build this bridge. For instance, a student has a story about camping. She wants to focus on seeing a bear for the first time with her friends. She listened to the previous lesson and applied it. Now all the boring bits about an irrelevant hide-and-seek game that did not develop character and had lots of detail about setting up tents and what have you that doesn't move the plot because it won't ever be connected to seeing the bear, are gone. It was a page worth of detail that was going nowhere. But she is stuck now. She can't find a bridge. Show her how to turn to a mentor text for help; there are many different examples of well-crafted time compression in *White Water*. Show her how Jonathan and Aaron London write:

> Over the next five river days we crashed through rapids, sat around the fire, ate great food, and slept under a billion bright stars.

The authors compressed five days into one sentence. She only needs to compress an hour. She should be able to come up with something like, "We played hide and seek for an hour while my parents set up the tents and got dinner started."

Reading Workshop Support

Have students notice time compression in their independent reading. Add to your chart all the interesting ways they find that writers compress time. How much time is compressed into how many sentences?

Homework Support

Ask students to go back in their writers' notebook and look for previous entries where time compression can be used to improve the pacing.

Related Readings

After the End, by Barry Lane (1993), pages 75–79, "Shrink a Century"
Craft Lessons, by Ralph Fletcher and Joann Portalupi (1998), page 31, "Time Transitions"

Wondrous Words, Katie Wood Ray (1999), pages 177–178, "Sentences That Make a Long
   Story Short"

LESSON 3: EXPLODE THE MOMENT

Components: Content and Craft
Mentor Texts Used: "Gimmetheball" from *Rimshots* (1999) by Charles R. Smith Jr., *White
Water* (2001) by Jonathan and Aaron London, *Wilma Unlimited* (2000) by Kathleen Krull
Previous Lessons/Background Knowledge Needed: Students need a sense of beginning,
middle, and end of a story. This is the sense of plot that you'll need to have been working
on through the reading connection in your reading workshop. Students need to understand
that after the buildup, there is a climax or turning point that is the focal event of the story
where the reader expects to spend some time, not be rushed through.

Lesson Introduction

I found the concept of Explode the Moment in Barry Lane's *After the End* (1993)—a very, very
helpful book that I use and read again and again. In it, he attributes the term *explode a moment* to Ilene Wax, a reading teacher from Halifax, Vermont. Wherever it originated from, I
know across my literacy initiative, it is widely used. I would like you to consider the exploded
moment through the pacing lens, because that's what it is, a pacing tool. Our students are
working to manage the pacing of their short stories, they need to first understand that readers expect the turning point of a short story to slow down, showing the significance of that
point. Then our students need a strategy, a tool to slow the pace.

   You could consider doing this lesson before Cut the Irrelevant and Time Compression, but
I prefer to do it after. It's easier for students to just work with what is relevant and build it up,
rather than search for the relevant, build it up, and cut the irrelevant later.

   Tell your students you know they have shrunken pieces now. This happens after cutting the
irrelevant and using time compression. Tell them not to worry, you have a lesson planned to
help them make their writing wonderful.

   First, remind students that writers *control* the flow of their piece, the big pacing. Say, "As
writers, you decide which parts to take your reader quickly through using time compression
and now you need to decide where to slow down. You time compressed the parts that aren't
so important, but now you need to stretch out the part or parts that are very important. Think,
how long do you want your reader to linger in this or that spot in your story? And why? Your
main idea will help you figure out where you should slow down your story."

   Then you'll need to really teach it. If you've got your own piece of writing going, you can
model your process and discuss your product. Or choose from the following ideas. I find exploding moments, first recognizing the moment and then really making that important moment stand out, is very difficult for most students. And I tell them so, then I try to help, as
concretely as I can.

Using a Visual

You'll need some modeling clay. Commend your students for working hard to cross out the irrelevant parts of their pieces and on deciding what the focus or main idea of their piece is. Show them a three-inch by five-inch flattish rectangle of modeling clay with bits sticking out of it. Use knowledge of students' pieces to talk about how one student crossed out this irrelevant part (remove a bit of sticking-out clay), and how another student crossed out this irrelevant part (continue to remove bits while quoting student examples until bits are gone). This shows them how the piece of writing is cleaned up now but is flat. Good writing is not flat; good writing has depth and detail. I like to refer them to a chart on this point for a visual reference such as the chart below.

FIG. 7.6

One way writers add more detail is by exploding the important moment(s) in the piece.

You can continue to use this modeling clay prop as a visual to support further work in later big pacing lessons: developing character, creating settings, whatever you see your students need. With the clay, you can help them see a well-paced piece is layered with purposeful detail because the reader wants and expects depth. As you talk about what they need to develop in their stories, add another layer of clay representing each lesson until you eventually get a rectangular prism.

Using Mentor Texts

I read aloud "Gimmetheball" by Charles R. Smith Jr. (1999). The whole thing is one big exploded moment. I ask my students to time how long it takes me to read the narrative and I point out the actual time that passes in the narrative is only seven or eight seconds. This obvious example helps them to see how they can and should slow the pace of their writing for the reader, and not rush their important moments. I also use *Wilma Unlimited* by Kathleen Krull (2000).

The most important moment, when Wilma takes off her leg brace and walks through the church, is slowed over pages in obvious contrast to other parts of the book where many years pass in time compression. I take the exploded moment and show my students how I can ruin it and the pacing by changing all that detail into one sentence. I rewrite it into the air: "Then Wilma took off her brace and walked through the church." When you do example, nonexample you give your students a better idea of what they are stretching for.

Any one of your favorite narrative picture books will have at least one exploded moment. Share it, discuss it, rewrite into one sentence. Be sure to chart your student's noticings about how that exploded moment effects the piece. And then compare, are similar writers' strategies used to compose the exploded moments in other favorite books? You may notice things like:

- Time seems to be slowed down and so much is written about just a moment of time.
- The writers have described feelings, sensory details, physical movements, and thoughts.
- The pacing is slowed so to give the reader the time to enjoy the most important in the piece in great detail.

Now take the step from the mentor texts to their own writing. Have your students look in their writing considering first what is the main idea; their main idea is their guide to the moment that would best be exploded. Is there that one sentence that best expresses their main idea, that could be exploded? "Then I made the basket. " Then finally got to ride the roller coaster." "Then I was skating." Have them find it. Now model on a chart or in your draft, if you have one, lifting that line out of the story and writing it on a fresh notebook page or draft paper. The single sentence, "Then I fell off my bike" could turn into a half page of painful slow motion. You will want to "write" some examples into the air to get them thinking about possibilities then:

- Have them take a minute to make a final decision on a sentence in their notebooks or drafts that they will lift.
- Ask for a student to share his or her one line.
- Take that line and write an exploded moment into the air, ask your students to help you.

- Pretend to be stuck and refer to a mentor text for help. For instance, notice the sensory detail in the mentor writing, then add it to your "in the air" writing. Or notice the mentor exploded moment is really long and add more to yours.
- Do a few more examples into the air from students' lifted lines until they look ready to try their own.
- Have them turn and talk out their exploded moment before you send them off to write.
- Discuss struggles and successes in closure; especially discuss the process of using the mentor text to help themselves.

Looking at Student Writing

Ricardo was a language learner. He spoke Spanish at home, in the classroom, and on the play yard. He wanted to explode the most important moment in his piece about learning to swim but was having trouble knowing what write. I asked him this series of questions in a conference to help him get back to that moment in the pool.

- What were you doing with your legs, arms?
- What were you trying to do to save yourself?
- How did it feel?
- What were you thinking during this moment?

Ricardo was then able to revise the most important moment in his piece when his brother saving him from drowning (see his first draft in Figure 7–7, then his revised draft in Figure 7–8).

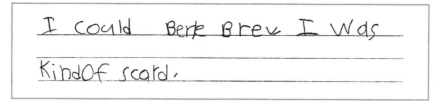

FIG. 7.7 *I could barely breathe. I was kind of scared.*

(Ricardo's entire piece appears in Chapter 11, Language Learners and Reading Like a Writer.)

Asking questions, as I did for Ricardo, is a helpful tool for writers who are having a tough time flushing out that exploded moment. You can explicitly teach your students this tool to help each other bring memories of specific detail back in focus so they can write about them. You are also reminding them about audience—that they write for a reader who expects a lot of details, especially at the most important point in a story. Note: I use this strategy in informational writing as well, and in developing snapshots (Lane 1993; see also my Advanced Small Pacing Lessons, Chapter 10). We don't have time to confer with each student when he or she needs help, we need to teach each student writer how to help themselves and each other.

I could hardly touch the bottom of the pool with my toes. I wanted to touch the wall but I couldn't. Water went into my mouth. I was scared. Then my brother saved me. He pulled my arm up and picked me up and got me out of the pool.

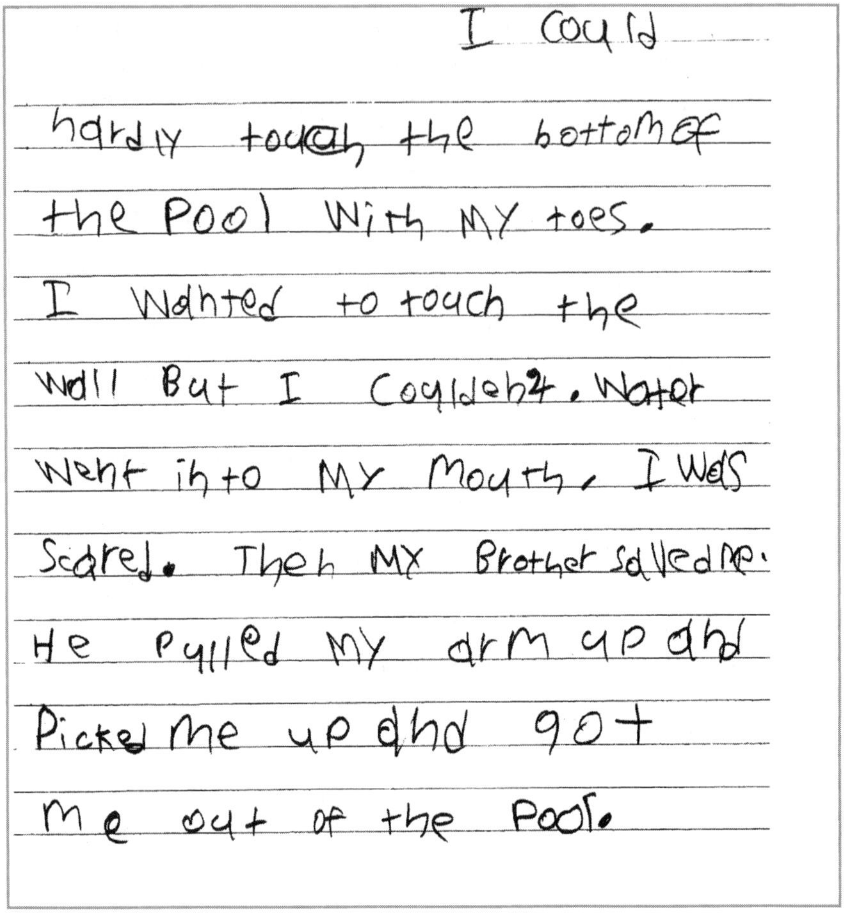

I could
hardly touch the bottom of
the Pool With MY toes.
I Wanted to touch the
wall But I couldebt. Water
Went into MY Mouth. I Was
Scared. Then MY Brother saved me.
He Pulled MY arm up and
Picked me up and got
me out of the Pool.

FIG. 7.8

Reading Workshop Support

Ask students to be on the lookout for exploded moments in their independent reading. Where does the writer slow things down for the reader and why, how do they do it and what are they describing through thoughts, feelings, or actions? Add additional noticings to your on-going chart.

Homework Support

Have students practice writing exploding moments. They need a lot of practice because they tend to write them too short. Have them continue to practice the "lift a line" strategy in their writers' notebooks.

Related Readings

After the End, by Barry Lane (1993), Chapter 5

Craft Lessons, by Ralph Fletcher and Joann Portalupi (1998), page 97, "Slowing Down the Hot Spot"

LESSON 4: LIST STRATEGY

Component: Content

Mentor Texts Used: *Thundercake* (1990) by Patricia Polacco

Previous Lessons/Background Knowledge Needed: This lesson is meant to help students who have a fairly strong basic piece of writing, with a strong beginning and middle including the use of time compression and an exploded moment, but the piece seems to end too abruptly.

Lesson Introduction

Good pacing needs to be controlled and sustained throughout the piece to the end. Many times we see student writing where the student seems to have run out of steam, wrapping up their story with "That was the best day ever." And a "The End" just to let you know they are quite done.

After spending time carefully crafting the pacing of their pieces with relevant detail, time compression, and an exploded moment, it would be a shame to end abruptly, to dump their reader off the raft.

If you have it or can get it, have a look in the *NCEE New Standards: Reading and Writing Grade by Grade* (1999) book, page 209–210, at the third grade narrative paper, "When my Puppys Ranaway." (Spelling errors are the student writer's.) This is a smoothly paced emotional piece. It flows beautifully until the end when the writer ends abruptly with "I've got over them leaving because mom says we can get 2 new puppys very soon." Of course this is a young writer, and a very fine at-standard narrative for a third grader. I like to show it to my students in our pacing work because the ending is so obviously abrupt. It raises their awareness to hold on to their pacing control all the way through to the end of their pieces.

When I noticed my students' pieces were ending with a simple reflective comment, I stopped to study what was happening. I looked again at a few favorite touchstones and I began to see that endings start much earlier then the very end of the story. The ending is the resolution element of a story, and readers don't like to feel rushed or dumped.

Using a Mentor Text

You certainly could do a guided inquiry, asking students to think about where an ending actually starts in their favorite books. You could make all sorts of charts and draw all sorts of conclusions and have them discover the craft that writers use to control the ending pacing of their pieces. But there is a great strategy in Patricia Polacco's *Thundercake*, I call it the List Strategy. And for teaching just this one strategy out of one book, direct teaching is effective.

Draw a story arc and plot out the events in Patricia Polacco's *Thundercake*. (See Figure 7–9 for an example story arc.) You can make the chart ahead of time, or draw it out while you talk through it.

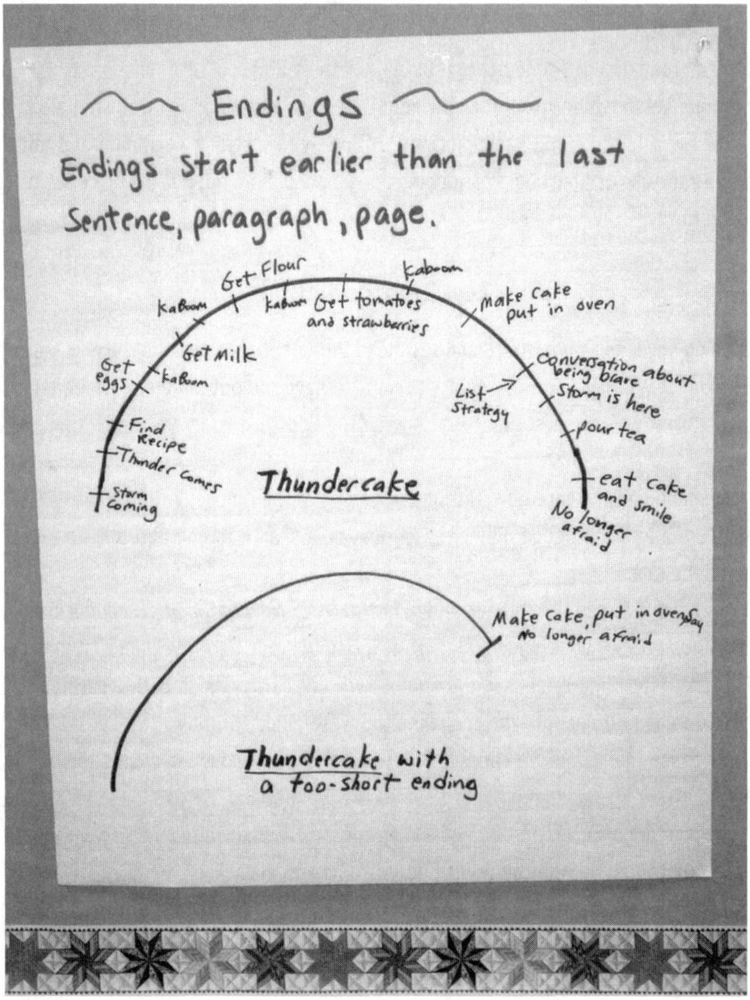

FIG. 7.9

Reread the last sentence in *Thundercake* but point out that it is not really the ending. The ending starts a few pages back with the grandmother and grandchild having a conversation and reflecting on how the grandchild was no longer afraid of thunder, how she was actually brave. The grandmother made her point by listing all the things that her granddaughter had done:

you got eggs from mean old Nellie Peck Hen,
you got milk from old Kick Cow,
you went through Tangleweed Woods to the dry shed,
you climbed the trellis in the barnyard.

This list marks the beginning of the resolution, which is quite slowly paced. Over a few more pages, they enjoyed tea and cake before the concluding last sentence. Draw another arc for *Thundercake* like the first but end it abruptly, cutting pages of detail that is in Polacco's resolution, including the list. Students need to see the difference. It's a great idea to do an example/nonexample like this whenever possible to help with meaning construction. Show them how Polacco used the list strategy to help slide the reader out of her story, to slow the pace and not end the story too soon.

Of course, not every student will want to use the list strategy to effectively pace the resolution to his or her stories. And you don't want your students to appear to have formulaic writing. The list strategy is just one idea. The big learning for your students is that the writer has to pace the resolution to avoid an abrupt ending. Now that students see the need to carefully and purposefully pace their endings, you can have your students do inquiry work into other ways to slide a reader out of their stories.

Looking at Student Writing

The students that I have seen choosing to use this list strategy are the ones writing a memoir about getting over fears or a first-time situation. They have a piece that they see (after this lesson) ends abruptly and they revise it by making up a conversation between themselves and another character in their memoir and inserting the conversation to slow the pace of the resolution. Yes, they make it up. Didn't someone say that memoir is fictionalized truth? I tell my students somebody did and as writers they owe it to their readers to deliver a well-paced piece. If that means making up a conversation, then that's what writers do. Many of my students use the list strategy successfully. Here is one example.

Priya, a third grader, was not happy with her abrupt and simple ending to her memoir, "Bear Watching." I remember her first draft going something like this:

After a while the bear ran away into the woods. From that time on I never feared of seeing a bear again.

Although I had taught the list strategy earlier in the week, she hadn't tried it yet like many of the other students had. We give our students so much information, so much to try. They are not all ready at the same time. In our conference, Priya and I sat in front of the chart and reviewed the idea of where an ending can actually start. She decided the list strategy would work for her. She decided to fictionalize the truth in order to improve her piece. She made up a conversation with her dad, artfully starting with a circle-back to the sound of crows that she had cawing at the beginning of her piece (see Figure 7–10).

After a while the bear ran away into the woods.

When I was going back to the van I heard the crows again, "Caw . . . caw . . . caw . . . ," they said.

As we drove out of the area, I said to my dad, "Daddy, I'm still scared of a brown bear."

"No you are not, you came out of the van and saw bear, you were not screaming when you saw the bear, you didn't run away when you saw the bear either. You are brave!" my dad said.

He was right. I was brave! We happily drove away. From that time on I never feared of seeing a bear again!

After a while the bear ran away into the woods.
When I was going back to the van I heard the crows again, "Caw... caw... caw...," they said.
As we drove out of the area, I said to my dad, "Daddy I'm still scared of a brown bear."
"No you are not, you came out of the van and saw bear, you were not screaming when you saw the bear, you didn't run away when you saw the bear either. You are brave!" my dad said.
He was right. I was brave! We happily drove away. From that time on I never feared of seeing a bear again!!!

FIG. 7.10

She was successful. And she was learning what writing a personal narrative can be. Not just a recording of what a writer remembers happening, but a carefully crafted well-paced piece to be enjoyed by a reader who expects craft and expects well-controlled pacing.

Reading Workshop Support

Continue to raise students' awareness of how resolutions are crafted. You could continue using the story arc, charting the beginnings, middle, and endings of your read-alouds or your text book stories. You could add to a "Strategies for Crafting a Satisfying Resolution" chart. Or you could discuss endings informally, having students share what they noticed in the pacing of the resolutions in their independent reading. They may notice some resolution pacing that they don't care for as a reader, perhaps they will find pacing they think is too fast or too slow, making for wonderful discussions.

Homework Support

The big ideas here are the story arc and the pacing of the resolution. You could assign students to make an entry in their readers' notebooks—an arc where they plot out the events in their most recently finished independent reading chapter book and note where they noticed the resolution begins.

LESSON 5: PURPOSEFUL USE OF DIALOGUE

Components: Content, Craft, and Conventions

Mentor Texts Used: *The Paperboy* (1996) by Dav Pilkey, *My Rotten Redheaded Older Brother* (1994) by Patricia Polacco, *Owl Moon* (1987) by Jane Yolen and study stacks of favorite narratives

Previous Lessons/Background Knowledge Needed: Use Lesson 4, List Strategy, for reference. Knowing the term "quotation marks." Some knowledge of the words *indent* and *paragraph.*

Lesson Introduction

This is a series of lessons to be given over three consecutive days. You are building a complex understanding of a difficult idea—purposeful, carefully-crafted dialogue. Hence the need for a three-day string of lessons. First day is guided inquiry to find the purpose of dialogue. Second day is to tackle the strange conventions that are how we punctuate dialogue. Third day is inquiry into dialogue attributions.

Students seem to want to include dialogue in their narratives with no thought for purpose. "Yes!" I said. "OK!" he said. "Let's go!" she said.

Useless dialogue is tiresome. It does not do the job that dialogue is supposed to do—to develop character and move the plot forward. Useless dialogue distracts the reader, ruining pacing. We need to help our students understand the purpose of dialogue: when to use it and just as importantly, when not to.

However, writing well-crafted, purposeful dialogue is very difficult. If you Google "writing dialogue" you will find many sites full of discussion about just how difficult it is, even for professional writers.

As this is a beginning lesson, for young, beginning writers, I simply open the door of inquiry into what purposeful dialogue looks and sounds like. As always, when students are given the opportunity to notice and to ask questions, they begin to understand, envision, and apply.

Day One, Useless Dialogue: Using Mentor Texts

I don't even bother to point out that the dialogue I see in their writing is useless, tiresome, pacing-ruining. They will discover that truth for themselves when they reread their pieces after doing guided inquiry about dialogue.

Pass out study stacks of picture book narratives to your small groups or partners. Ask the students to find and notice dialogue, and to note when in the story does it occur and why and how much? What are the characters talking about? How do the conversations help you understand who the characters are? What do the conversations do for the story? What more do you know after you read the dialogue? They'll need to use sticky notes to mark the dialogue they are studying and have a piece of paper to take notes. Make sure you include copies of *The Paperboy*, which has no dialogue. *Owl Moon* is also a good choice as there is almost no dialogue. Or, find some other well-crafted quiet books like Rylant's *When I Was Young in the Mountains* because you also want to make the point that narratives don't *require* dialogue.

After giving plenty of time to study the narratives and take notes, have a discussion and make a noticing chart. Guide them minimally. Let them figure it out. As always, there are no right or wrong answers, you are just looking to chart what makes sense. But there are some points to guide them to, to nudge their thinking, like:

- Why is there no or almost no dialogue in some of the texts we studied?
- What would happen to the story if there were dialogue?

When your discussion is complete, it is likely that everything you wrote down that they noticed can be reworded into either "advance the plot" or "develop character." Use these expressions. Ask them to envision using purposeful dialogue in their writing or none at all.

Make a final point by picking up a copy of a mentor text and rewriting it into the air with useless dialogue, then ask them what you have done to the pace. When your discussion is finished for the day, send them back to their seats to apply their new learning, to notice the clunking of their useless dialogue and make their revisions.

Day Two, Punctuation: Using Mentor Texts

Readers need correct punctuation to make sense of dialogue. And although the punctuation rules around dialogue don't make sense, we have to teach them anyway. I lean on guided inquiry. I like to use Patricia Polacco's *My Rotten Redheaded Older Brother* as a mentor text because the dialogue content is engaging. Your students can easily envision writing a dialogue fight scene like the one in Polacco's book because they've all had them in real life. Polacco's book shows them how to punctuate dialogue correctly so the reader knows who is talking without a he or she said after each line. The fight scene example shows that whenever a new person speaks, a new paragraph is started:

"Bet I can pick more blackberries than you can," he jeered at me one day.
"No you can't."
"Can so."
"Cannot!"
"Can," he whispered.

"Not," I said louder.

"Can!" he whispered so low that I could hardly hear him.

We study this fight scene and decide the author shouldn't go more than four times without identifying the speaker so the reader won't get confused. Of course, Hemingway has two characters go on for pages with no dialogue tags in *Farewell to Arms*, but they don't need to know that.

As a class, we make up a punctuation-in-dialogue chart with all the conventions that we notice in our reading like a writer work and include examples to give a visual to the conventions.

And as to the commas where you might expect periods, and the general difficulty in punctuating dialogue, I tell my students: refer to the chart when editing and remember to get extra help by picking up a mentor text and eventually you'll internalize the conventions. Directing your students to mentor texts is a solid step toward making them more independent in developing their editing skills. They need to see dialogue convention rules in use in writing in order to make sense of them.

Day Three, Dialogue Attributions: Using Mentor Texts

It is important for your students to understand the purpose of different kinds of dialogue attributions. Guide them to see how *writers* manage identifying the speaker and the speaker's tone. Your students will find it is not by referring to a chart of "Words to Use Instead of *Said*."

Study your picture books, you will see plenty of just *said* and *asked*. You will also see *said* with adverbs attached and words other than *said* or *asked*. But there is not a lot of writing in a picture book and therefore the tags are sometimes used to move the plot forward or develop character. Students need to see the thoughtful purpose in when to choose *said* or *asked* and when to elaborate.

You may want to take the time to help them understand that *said* and *ask* are most preferred by fine writers because they are transparent. Have a look through longer books, chapter books. If the writer takes the time to develop the character, a scene, then dialogue attributions other than *said* and *asked* are not necessary because the reader already knows how the dialogue should be read by knowing the character. Annoying dialogue attributions like *chortled* and *quipped* or *he said expectantly* and *she answered hesitantly* will bog down the pacing and will cause the reader to go back and reread the line of dialogue with a chortle or a quip. A fine writer will have described the character and scene well enough beforehand so you won't need the word *chortle* to know how the dialogue should sound.

I recently read a fourth-grade student's writing where there was an adverb tagged to the end of every single *he said* or *she said*. And there was a lot of dialogue. It was annoying. It was apparent that the student writer was depending entirely on his adverbs to develop character because there wasn't much of any other character development. A teacher-led inquiry into what writers actually do would help this student writer construct a more smoothly paced piece.

Reading Workshop Support

Amazingly, where students never noticed dialogue in a writerly way, they will now. Purposeful dialogue is a difficult concept and deserves more discussion and processing time. I like to use reading textbooks, a good source of multiple copies of the same text, so we can all ponder the same piece of writing and learn more together. Later, students will start to bring *you* interesting dialogue that they find in their independent reading.

Homework Support

Students need a lot of practice with our strange way of punctuating dialogue. You could strengthen the good-writers-notice-the-world-around-them habit, have them listen in on conversations and record them in their writers' notebooks, practicing the punctuation and new paragraph for a new speaker conventions.

Related Readings

On Writing—A Memoir of the Craft (2000), by Stephen King, pages 119–121
For quotation marks, see *Grammatically Correct*, by Anne Stilman, pages 172–175, check the
    index for other pages around dialogue
After the End (1993), by Barry Lane, pages 59–63

Other Lesson Ideas in Basic Big Pacing

- Continue to explore the ways writers bring resolution to their writing. You may find other specific strategies you can label, like we did the List Strategy, adding to possible variations to pace an ending to a piece.
- Have students circle blocks of writing on their drafts that are the beginning, middle, and end. How is the balance? How much writing is in each block?
- Use any other lesson that will support students with their need to understand basic big pacing based on what you see in ongoing assessment of their writing in relation to the standards, or what you are passionate about teaching, or what they have expressed interest in learning.

Basic Small Pacing Lessons

This chapter contains basic small pacing lessons that are focused primarily around sentence control. I have arranged them in the order I have always presented them, but you may find that a different order will work better for your students. I have discovered that they are best done in a set, a string of lessons that will help your students build meaning around control and purpose of their sentence length and structure.

These lessons will often follow some basic narrative big pacing work that I have already done. And in that case, students will have some sort of draft for sentence revision work. But I prefer to start these lessons before they are too far into revising their drafts because these are important skills to keep in mind when rewriting. These small-pacing strategies support the rhythm and flow of big pacing, and your students need an understanding of both big and small pacing to eventually be able to write fluent, well-crafted, well-paced pieces.

BASIC SMALL PACING LESSONS LIST

1. Noticing Variety in Sentence Lengths (or, Counting Words)
2. Long Sentences and Run-ons
3. Short Sentences and Fragments
4. Beginning to Explore Sentence Structure and Formalizing Inquiry Steps (This is also good one to use to help them start to craft a lead for a well-paced beginning.)
5. Punctuation Study #1

LESSON 1: NOTICING VARIETY IN SENTENCE LENGTHS

Components: Content and Craft
Mentor Texts Used: *Before the Storm* (1995), by Jane Yolen, "Gimmetheball" (1999), by Charles R. Smith
Previous Lessons/Background Knowledge Needed: Preread *Before the Storm* or some other simple, slowly paced small moment narrative. Cynthia Rylant's *When I was Young in*

the Mountains is another good choice. It is a series of vignettes, but more importantly for our purposes here, it is slowly paced. Make sure you have read it to your class at once already, just for enjoyment. Also be sure to have read "Gimmetheball" to your students, or some other very intense fast-paced narrative that reads in sharp contrast to your slow narrative. Otherwise, no previous lessons needed.

Lesson Introduction

Small pacing strategies support big pacing strategies. If you have noticed that a particular narrative moves along lazily, then you have probably noticed long and complex sentence structure in that narrative.

If you have noticed that a particular narrative moves along quickly, then you have probably noticed shorter sentence structure.

If you have noticed the pace changes in a narrative from slow to fast to slow again, then you have probably noticed the matching change in sentence structure.

A writer will decide on slowing or quickening the pace of his or her writing depending on what pace would best match and support the content of the piece. We see the craft of the sentence length and structure supporting that big pacing choice. Of course, other things, like word choice and conventions, add to pacing control in sentences. We'll start here in the basic small pacing lessons with sentence length.

This first lesson is meant to raise your students' awareness that there are choices writers make in sentence length and there is purpose behind those choices.

Each student will need their own narrative they have finished or are close to finishing, that is, they'll need more than just a paragraph to work with. I like to use their beginning-of-the-year on-demand personal narrative writing prompt that is required in our literacy initiative at the beginning, middle, and end of the year. Using their prompt makes the point that they should always be thoughtful of how they construct their writing, be it a one-hour prompt, or a piece that is weeks into the writing process. They could also use a lengthy writer's notebook narrative entry. But they do need something of their own writing.

Using Mentor Texts

If you'd like, you can reinforce the river metaphor here. You might begin by reminding your students, When you read a piece of writing, you can think of it as floating on a raft down a river. Sometimes your ride on the river will be slow and peaceful, like we find in the pacing in Jane Yolen's *Before the Storm*. Your raft will float lazily along on smooth water, past interesting and beautiful river banks and around a bend or two until you softly drift over to the edge of the river and step out of your raft at the end of the book.

Or, you continue, your raft may move quickly along a more rushing river, like in Charles R. Smith's "Gimmetheball." It's not a scary-fast ride, but it is fast, and you hang on to the edges of your raft as you quickly move around one bend and then another until the force of the water pushes you over to the river bank at the end of the story.

Ask students to listen again to the slowness of Jane Yolen's *Before the Storm* and the fast pace of "Gimmetheball" as you read aloud. Read the first part of each text, read them very well; students need to hear the difference in the pacing, the difference in your breathing.

Tell them, As the writer you control the river ride for your reader. You make the pacing decisions, you decide many things that help to control your pacing in your piece, and one of the decisions you make is about the length of your sentences. Then ask students to do the following:

■ As you read Yolen's *Before the Storm* (or your similar book) out loud sentence by sentence, have them keep track of the number of words in each sentence. On chart paper, you record the numbers they give you in a vertical line on one side of your chart. Go as far into the book as you need to go to make your point. Save some space at the bottom of the chart to record noticings.

■ Read "Gimmetheball" (or your similar text) the same way, record the number of words in each sentence in a vertical line on the other side of your chart.

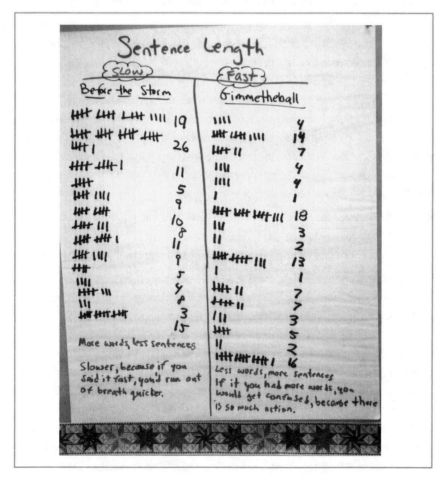

FIG. 8.1

- Compare, discuss, and record their noticings. Discuss how authors vary their sentence lengths, but slower pieces have longer sentences overall and faster pieces have shorter sentences overall.
- Next, return their prompts or some other narrative they have written along with a strip of scratch paper. Have them count the number of words in every one of their sentences. They love to do this, counting their words, the whole room is quietly humming with numbers. Come together as a group to share their findings. If your class is like my class at the beginning of the year, your students will be finding they have no control at all, and they are actually laughing at their forty-seven- and sixty-four-word sentences. Other students may have droning writing with sentences all about the same length, usually between seven and ten words. Some find they have no periods at all. (If you see a lot of that, no periods, jump next to the Punctuation Study Lesson #1.) This exercise is an eye-opener for students, and stresses that writers are expected to gain control and have purpose when crafting sentence length.

Now you have another decision to make: what to do with their writing time and how to scaffold what you'd like them to do. It's tricky because all you've done is raise their awareness that they need sentence length variety. You are not completely into purpose of sentences length as tied to the content of a piece quite yet. You are building toward that.

Probably the best way to proceed is to model what you expect. Have an already chosen piece of student writing (something you spotted yesterday and asked the student's permission to use) copied up on chart paper or ready for your overhead. Using this piece of writing you are going to think out loud and model the process. Before you do this, though, you first need to think about what most of your students need and what can they handle. Teach to just that one thing for now. In modeling, you could choose to focus on:

- How to listen for the end of a sentence so periods can be placed
- How to combine sentences
- How to cut out extra words to find those short sentences that are buried in there

It is best to teach just one of these points at a time. Teach many things at once and your students will likely get nothing. Of course there are exceptions, but this basic lesson on sentence length, foundational to building meaning around sentence purpose and variety, is not the place to give your students too much to consider all at once.

After your whole-class lesson around one thing, you might pull together a small group of students with similar needs. If you addressed the needs of most of your students by modeling sentence combining, but a percentage still need help finding the ends of sentences they have, or visa versa, pull that small group together and teach to what they need most now.

With your modeling scaffold in place, ask students to revise notebook entries or drafts with thought toward controlling sentence length. You could even photocopy their prompts and let them experiment with revision work. More learning will happen in closure of this lesson and in the following lessons in this string.

When you gather for closure, prompt them to use the language of writers and begin to nudge them toward understanding the purpose of sentence length choices: "I revised/wrote this entry from long sentences into mostly short ones because it is about when I was winning a race and I wanted to use the fast pace of short sentences like in 'Gimmetheball' to support my content." If they can't quite say that, you restate their attempts for them: "I hear you saying . . ." until they can articulate it on their own. They should be learning to talk about strategy, purpose, and mentor text. Once they can label it, it's internalized.

Using Your Own Writing

After the counting words lesson, I do a different version of this lesson, but the next day. It continues to help build students' understanding for this important aspect of pacing in writing.

The two mentor texts used in the previous lesson, one fast-paced, one slow, gave them a clear contrast to help with meaning construction. In this version, give them contrasting examples, but not a fast-paced to slow-paced example. Build on the concept of sentence length variety. First choose between a slowly paced or faster piece to show them, whichever you choose to write and share, but make it obvious. And be careful, make sure your writing sounds like theirs in sentence length, complexity, and level of vocabulary. I wrote a slowly paced piece as an example, but as you'll see later I had trouble with the level of sophistication.

The plan here with your writing is to give students a visual aide. Example, nonexample. You want them to clearly see the difference between a piece with sentences all similar in length and one with sentence length variety. Write your short piece, carefully varying your sentence lengths with purpose toward your pacing. Then, rewrite your piece making all the sentences similar in length. Show them the same-length one first. If you write it with each of your similar-length sentences on separate lines, they will more easily see the sameness. If you read it with your body rocking to the droning beat, and ask them to join you, they will get it kinesthetically.

Here's my droning version:

One day I went to my grandmother's house.
My hair was long and straight and I wanted curly hair.
I asked my grandmother if she would curl my hair.
She said, "Of course, I would love to curl your hair."
She got out an old basket of pink, plastic curlers.
First she brushed my hair to get out the tangles.
Then she put a big blue towel on my shoulders.
She got a water spray bottle and sprayed my hair.
I could feel my hair get heavier as she sprayed it.
Then she started to roll my hair up in the curlers.
After a very long time she was finally finished.
Then I waited for a long time for my hair to dry.

When my hair was dry she removed the curlers.
For about a few hours my long hair had curls.
Then my hair started to straighten out again.
She said, "Oh well, they were lovely for awhile."
But I wanted the curls to stay and I was very sad.

Show them your revised version, also written sentence by sentence to make your point visually. Talk about the choices you made, not only in varying your sentence lengths, but also talk about your purpose. I talk about how I not only wanted sentence length variety so the writing would sound good to the reader, but also how I mostly wanted long sentences because I want my reader's breathing to be soft, the way mine is when I think of this memory. I don't want quick breathing—that would appropriate for different content. I want a thoughtful, slow kind of pace that matches my content.

Here's my sentence length variety version:

When I was young my hair was very long and very straight.

I wanted curly hair.

One day, when I was visiting my grandmother, I asked her if she would curl my hair.

"Of course, dear," she said.

I followed her as she went into her bathroom, reached up to a high cabinet and carefully got down an old basket of pink, plastic curlers.

She asked me to stand in front of the bathroom mirror.

I watched her hands working gently as she carefully and slowly brushed my hair to get out all the tangles.

Then she put a big blue towel on my shoulders.

I watched her get a water spray bottle and spray my hair until it was heavy and dripping.

Slowly, she began to roll up my hair into the curlers, first one and then another, and another, and another until finally she was finished.

I waited for hours for my hair to dry.

As she carefully removed the curlers I saw I had the hair I wanted, beautiful curls falling around my face and neck, across my shoulders and down my back.

For a few hours the curls held.

Then they started to droop and loosen themselves back to straight hair again.

I wanted them to stay forever.

Sad and disappointed, I looked at my grandmother.

"Oh well," she said, "they were lovely for awhile.

We'll do it again someday."

Let me stop here and continue my point about using your own writing. The most important thing is you experience and learn the process and can therefore discuss and confer authentically about choices you make as a writer with your students, about the struggles you had. "We write so we can explain it all," says Katie Wood Ray (2002), the difficulty is you may be writing over your students' heads. I wrote these sentence length examples when I was teaching in fourth grade. I know they don't work well in my third grade classrooms, they're only good as a visual aide. I know the content is accessible, but the sentences are too long and complex. So if I begin to talk about sentence structure choices, students likely won't understand, at least not at this point in the year. These examples barely worked with my fourth graders.

I need to write up another set. To do that in a manner that will help my third grade students, I need to study a piece of beginning-of-the-year, droning third grade writing and imitate it for sentence length and structure. Then rewrite it being careful not to stretch out of the grade level. And someday I will do that. In the meantime, I show them the difference between my two pieces, and I have them count words in sentences. I know that works very well.

Reading Workshop Support

This is where having those reading textbooks to pass out so everyone has a copy of the same mentor text comes in handy. Read and discuss writers' choices toward sentence length in relation to pacing speed and in relation to content. Reaffirm that even in generally slow or generally fast-paced pieces, there is still variety in sentence length to support flow and rhythm.

Homework

Students will need to continue writing a new entry or draft or revising an old one with this lesson in mind. They will need a lot of practice to develop this skill. Have them share their thought processes the next day—using writerly language.

Related Readings

Craft Lessons, by Barry Lane (1993), page 85

Teaching the Qualities of Writing, by JoAnn Portalupi and Ralph Fletcher (2004), page L-14

6+1 Traits of Writing, by Ruth Culham (2003), page 200

Grammatically Correct, by Anne Stilman (1997), pages 308–309 for an excellent clarification of sentence length variety and purpose with audience and genre considerations

What You Know by Heart (2002), by Katie Wood Ray, Chapter 1

LESSON 2: LONG SENTENCES AND RUN-ONS

Components: Content and Craft

Mentor Text Used: Use any of your favorites

Previous Lessons/Background Knowledge Needed: An understanding of basic sentence structure, subject/predicate, some grammar work on the use of the conjunction *and*, and the difference between a long sentence and a run-on sentence.

Lesson Introduction

In the previous lesson, your students may have been laughing at their forty-seven- and sixty-four-word sentences. In this lesson, help them see that long sentences exist in good writing but they are carefully crafted with purpose.

Originally, I would copy long sentences of between twenty-one and ninety-five words out of the books I found them in, print them up each on a separate sheet of paper, distribute them around the room, and as a class we would consider the structure and purpose of just that sentence. My students would identify the purpose of sentences in isolation from the surrounding text. Purposes such as:

- To compare different things
- To describe something, using lots of detail
- To make a list of important things
- To show a lot of time passing

I have quite a collection of long sentences as students have brought new ones to me over the years as they find them in their independent reading. Gradually, I began to see that looking at a single sentence in isolation was not helpful. It was interesting, but of no use to students because they couldn't see what work that sentence was doing inside the text.

I find guided inquiry with study stacks is the best choice here to conduct this lesson, although you could certainly choose to show several examples in a direct lesson. I like guided inquiry because I am also doing the teaching and facilitating of getting students to think about and discuss writing and author's purpose, to begin to learn to read like writers. Later in the year they will be doing more of that on their own, but early in the year I need to give them guided opportunity. I want them not only to find long sentences but discover for themselves why an author used them as they did in a particular place in the text.

Using Mentor Texts

Distribute your narrative picture books that you know have long sentences. That should be just about every book you have. Working in pairs, have your students place sticky notes on their finds and discuss the author's purpose. Come together as a class and share noticings around long sentences. You and your class will build your own chart around your own developed understanding. Some of your noticings might be:

Long Sentences

- Help build rhythm to the sound of the writing when surrounded by short and medium sentences in texts like *White Water, Beekeepers, The Lotus Seed.*
- Slow the pace, giving lots of details and allowing the reader to linger in a scene in a moment of time before moving on in texts like *Going North, The Relatives Came, Come On, Rain!*

Give an anxious, out-of-control feeling, particularly if a run-on in a book like *The Lotus Seed* (and you must see the ninety-five-word sentence in *Joey Pigza Looses Control* (Gantos 2000), page 174). It is a perfect example of how a writer's craft supports content. A ninety-five-word run-on is exactly what the author, Jack Gantos, needs to show his ADHD character's desperate attempt to get away from his you-don't-need-meds dad and back into his mother's arms.

But don't tell your students, let them tell you.

In the months to come, you and your students will want to be able to refer back to the examples that you found and studied. You will need these mentor sentences for work in the writing that your students will be attempting over the year. "Where was that long sentence that slowed the scene using such detail, I want to do that in my writing too and I need to study it again." Create some kind of system, like noting the source of your examples on your chart, or some other notation for easily tracking down these examples when you need them.

Be sure students have time to try out long sentence writing in a new entry or in revision work in their writers' notebooks. In closure, they should share their thinking about the choices they made and tie their thinking back to the writers' language of your chart.

Looking at Student Writing

Third grader Mandeep learned the power of using run-ons to show anxiety. She applies that craft in the beginning of her narrative, as shown in Figure 8–2. She also uses an effective fragment to start with, which is the next lesson.

One hour, two hour and three hours to get to the Golden Gate Bridge. And my stomach started to hurt and my mom was driving and my dad was telling which way to go and my cousin was leading the way and finally my mom said, "We're here."

FIG. 8.2

Reading Workshop Support

Students should watch for long sentences in their independent reading. Have them share and discuss the author's purpose in closure. Add examples to your writing chart if you want to save them as a future resource.

Homework

Students should continue crafting long sentences with an identifiable purpose in mind. They need practice. Share successes, struggles, and purpose the next day.

Related Readings

6+1 Traits of Writing (2003), by Ruth Culham, Chapter 6: Sentence Fluency
Grammatically Correct (1997), by Anne Stilman, pages 306–308. A must read! (And she has my ninety-five-word example beat with a 202-word example from *Ulysses* by James Joyce.)
Wondrous Words (1999), by Katie Wood Ray, page 171, "Runaway Sentences"

LESSON 3: SHORT SENTENCES AND FRAGMENTS

Components: Content, Craft, and Conventions
Mentor Text Used: Examples are listed in Lesson Introduction section.
Previous Lessons/Background Knowledge Needed: An understanding of basic sentence structure, subject/predicate so students can talk about the difference between a short sentence and a fragment. This lesson works well as part of the string of lessons, following Lesson 2, Long Sentences and Run-ons.

Lesson Introduction

In the previous lesson you did inquiry work into long sentences. Today, help students use their growing strengths at reading like writers to do inquiry work into the purpose of short sentences and fragments. Throughout all these lessons you are building their awareness that writers make choices, purposeful choices. After first raising your students' awareness that indeed well-written writing has purposeful sentence length variety, and at times sentences are very long, but with purpose, now you can look at just short sentences and fragments. They will continue to learn that writers control their craft.

For this lesson, I like to photocopy some pages, maybe just three, from mentor texts where I have found short sentences and fragments. Some examples are:

Thundercake: There is a simple repeating three-word sentence: "I was scared." I like to use the page that has that sentence and also starts with, "Milk was next."
The first page of *Fishing Sunday*: "And still."
If you're feeling brave you could photocopy the first page of Andrew Clements' *Things Not Seen* (2004) and have a look at "I'm. Not. There." These short sentences finish a string of short, complete sentences in very short paragraphs.

Flipping through your favorite narratives will reveal short sentences and fragments, just like you found long sentences. Find examples you'd like to discuss. Or, have your students do the hunting through your study stacks.

Ideally, as you are looking through the books in your study stacks (remember the library as a resource) doing all this sentence length work, think about narrowing the stack. Eventually choosing a few favorite narratives that will be your touchstones that you and your class will refer to again and again studying them deeply for all the different craft they have. Those favorite books will be the ones you buy to keep.

Using Mentor Texts

There are three ways to use mentor texts with this lesson. You could use:

Direct Teaching

You could do a direct five- or ten-minute minilesson and point out where, when, and why short sentences or fragments are used. Use examples from books your students have already heard read aloud many times. Show them how writers use short sentences and fragments for emphasis.

Guided Inquiry with Preselected, Photocopied Examples

At your meeting area, pass out photocopied bits of text where you know students will find well-crafted short sentences and fragments. This preselected mentor text method is also a good idea if you have narrowed down the books you are studying in your genre study and you want the students to become very familiar with those few books. I like to do this preselected mentor method at the beginning of the year when students are just learning to read like writers. I like that they are all there with you at the meeting area, looking at the same texts because you can easily direct them if they get lost with, "Count the number of words in each sentence; do you find any that have five words or less? What is the author's purpose for such a short sentence right there?" As the teacher, to guide discussion, you should first have had a close look at the examples you chose. Notice what the writers have done with their short sentences and why. What is happening in the content of the piece when the short sentences or fragments are employed? Read the writing out loud and notice your breathing. What is happening to the mood, to the tone, to the pace of the narrative?

I have the students stay on the carpet in our meeting area and have a look at the text with a partner, first locating the short sentence or fragment in the text, then discussing author's purpose. It doesn't take too long, they're getting a little faster, feeling more empowered about noticing what writers do as we move through this string of lessons.

You can chart their comments and noticings when they are ready. And since they each have a copy of the text, everyone can look at the page being discussed and add more thoughts to the group discussion. I talk about this further later in the lesson.

But if you've just read this lesson this morning and your writing workshop starts in ten minutes, and you have no time to preselect texts, then do what I did the first time: skip to the next choice using study stacks, and have your students do all the work. Let them hunt for short sentences and fragments and discover the writers' purpose.

Guided Inquiry Using Study Stacks

Have study stacks of all your picture books, owned and/or borrowed, and just see how the treasure hunt goes. I like this method because the students, while digging through all those books, find things for me that I never knew were there and I can pick and choose the most powerful examples to return to, this year and in future years. They love finding examples that I have never seen.

Whether your students have looked through stacks or your preselected examples, you'll need to discuss and chart their thoughts. If my students had the word *emphasis*, they would use it in the discussion. I usually get a lot of words and phrases that mean *emphasis* until finally I commend them on the good thinking they have done, and I tell them there is one word for all they have said. Writers use short sentences and fragments for emphasis. Then I'll ask why did the writer chose not to emphasize this or that other sentence? And why didn't the writer make every sentence short? Why are there just a few fragments or none at all? And other nudging questions to push their thinking.

As a final thought-pushing, meaning-making exercise, you could rewrite some of the short sentences you found into longer ones, either right there on the chart, or into the air. Remember the power of example/nonexample. You could use Cynthia Rylant's *When I Was Young in the Mountains*, which finishes with her only short sentence in the entire book: "And that was always enough." Why didn't she write, "And when I think back about when I was young in the mountains I know that everything I had was enough for me"?

After the direct lesson or inquiry work, students will need time to write. Have them turn and talk with a partner first about a place in their writing where they might craft a short sentence or fragment for emphasis. This is the envisioning step to inquiry. It's a good idea to have their writing in front of them while they are considering revisions. Have them consider their purpose. Where in their own writing would it work best? Purposefully add emphasis? Be most powerful? You can excuse them to apply their new learning to their writing: to revise an already written piece in their writers' notebooks, or do a new piece of writing just to try out the craft, or do revision work in a draft. Share struggles and successes at closure. Encourage them to articulate purpose. If they are having trouble articulating, restate their efforts with writerly language: "I hear you saying. . . ."

Looking at Student Writing

I have seen students grow to understand this purposeful short sentences and fragments concept solidly. Later in the year, I'll continue to see short sentences and purposeful fragments in their writing even if we haven't discussed it in a long time and the chart is long covered up.

Third grader Jesus shows control over his sentence length and effective use of Andrew Clement's style fragments in his paragraph from his memoir about camping (see Figure 8–3). Actually, the revision suggestion was made to him in a response group. The other student writers remembered Clement's craft from earlier reading and thought Jesus' piece was a perfect

FIG. 8.3

I didn't believe him because usually he tricks me, so I went to take a look for myself. Then there it was. A big. Brown. Bear!

place for nonconventional use of conventions to support his content of being really scared of that bear. Jesus agreed and made his revisions, changing his fragment, *A big, brown bear!* to *A big. Brown. Bear!* If you are opening doors instead of setting ceilings, your students will learn to write well and with purpose. Certainly, in this example, Jesus looks like he is following the one rule of writing in my class: You may write anyway you would like to write, as long as it sounds like you know what you are doing.

Reading Workshop Support

Have students watch for short sentences and fragments in their independent reading. Share and discuss the author's purpose in the examples they find. Add examples to your writing chart if you want to save them as a future resource, especially if some slightly different purpose comes up.

Homework

Students should continue crafting short sentences and fragments and be able to articulate purpose the next day. Let them know what you will expect: articulation of purpose.

Related Readings

6+1 Traits of Writing (2003), by Ruth Culham, Chapter 6: Sentence Fluency
Grammatically Correct (1997), by Anne Stilman, pages 59, 262–263
After the End, by Barry Lane (1993), page 192, "Long sentence, short sentence"
Wondrous Words (1999), by Katie Wood Ray, page 172, "Artful Sentence Fragments"

LESSON 4: BEGINNING TO EXPLORE SENTENCE STRUCTURE AND FORMALIZING INQUIRY STEPS

Components: Content, Craft, Conventions
Mentor Text Used: *Before the Storm* (1995) by Jane Yolen, and *Owl Moon* (1987) by Jane Yolen

Previous Lessons/Background Knowledge Needed: An understanding of basic sentence structure, subject/predicate, so you will be able to talk about independent and dependent clauses; an understanding of verb tenses; series commas and the use of *and* in a series.

Lesson Introduction

This is a two-day lesson. It is not easy. It might be considered more advanced than basic. I have it here because I use it to begin to explicitly build students' reading like writer skills. I also have it here in basic lessons because I use it to help them to craft a strong beginning to a narrative, and I always teach crafting beginnings at the beginning of the school year. This lesson is meant to be taught after the all the previous lessons in sentence length and variety.

To prepare, I do some review in verb conjugation work first. In my word work time, I work up a verb tense chart from a whole-class discussion, accessing and adding to what they already know. I include basic verb tenses up to and including past participle. I am not going to quiz them on verb tenses, I am just offering some foundational pieces, some language of grammar to help them construct meaning in context in this lesson. The verb chart stays up all year as we frequently need to remind ourselves of the often peculiar ways our English language works.

Although it may appear, at least on the first day of this lesson, that I am teaching only one thing because we are looking to imitate only one particular sentence, actually four things are happening:

1. I am formally identifying the steps to inquiry; we've been informal up to now.
2. I am beginning to show them grammar of more complex sentence structures.
3. I am scaffolding toward learning what close imitation is.
4. Students are continuing to build their learning that different sentence structures provide different pacing and are appropriate for different content.

You will be explicitly showing students the steps that take them from reading writers' craft to trying it out in their own writing. I use Katie Wood Ray's steps of the inquiry process in this order:

1. Notice
2. Ask Questions
3. Label
4. Envision
5. Apply

I've been doing this informally with my students all along in previous lessons, since the first day of school. Now, with that schema of previous inquiry to build on, it's time to explicitly lay out the steps. I suppose I could have formally taught these steps from day one, but I like to ease into it because I am covering so much in writing at the beginning of the school year: rituals, routines, and so on, not to mention everything in all our other curricular areas. We'll get here, to formalizing the steps, easily within the first month of school. That's soon enough.

I will have made a small chart ahead of time with "Reading Like a Writer: The Inquiry Process" on the top of it, as a title. Under the title I have written the five steps so we can refer to them again and again until I see everyone has them internalized; only then does the little chart come down, and that might mean that it may stay up all year. I could choose to write an explanation alongside every step of the inquiry process, but I believe the chart would be too filled with words and would not serve its purpose, which is just to cue us as to what to do next. I will help them learn what each step means as we do this process together over and over again.

As an aside here, I eventually simplify the wording for the inquiry process down to a "magic three" that I hope my students will remember for the rest of their lives, three words rich with meaning and process: *Read. Learn. Apply.*

I hope they will remember this magic three like I remember "*i* before *e* except after *c*." Only that's not too helpful. And it speaks to all the rote learning of my early years instead of the real work of *thinking* that we should have been taught. That's okay, we can be proud that in teaching as a profession we are always looking to improve the work we do with our students. We've come a long way and I am sure we'll be going much farther.

Using Mentor Texts and Formally Labeling the Inquiry Process

I use the chart to talk about how we've been doing this five-step process already, and I tell them what a fine job they have been doing. I tell them now we'll explicitly think about the process of inquiry as we study one mentor sentence. It's a process that they will eventually learn to do on their own. And when they do the difficult but rewarding work of learning to read like a writer, they should know they are giving themselves a gift for life. A gift that will forever help them improve their writing skills. It's a little complicated, so for starters we will refer to the five steps on the chart one by one to remind us what to do and label what we are doing as we look at just the first sentence of *Before the Storm*. I'll write this sentence on chart paper (or write it ahead of time):

> It was a hot summer day, the air crackling with heat, and Strider lay panting by the barn door.

Then we return to our chart:

1. We choral read the sentence out loud and I ask students to *notice* what is happening in this sentence. We notice things like:

   The number of words
   The feel of the slow pace
   The two commas and the pause in your breathing that they require

2. We *ask questions* as to why Yolen crafted her sentence this way. What is the purpose? Have we seen this kind of sentence in other texts (yes! the first sentence of *Owl Moon* is constructed exactly the same way)? Was it serving the same

purpose? Why does Jane Yolen use the same sentence structure to start two different books? How does the structure of the sentence support the pacing? And is the pacing the same in her two books?

To help our thinking, I'll rewrite the sentence into three sentences so we can discuss the difference:

> It was a hot summer day.
> The air was crackling with heat.
> And Strider lay panting by the barn door.

We consider what I had to do to the words between the commas to change them into a complete sentence. We consider the different sound the writing has now, the different small pacing. That takes us to the next step.

3. We *label* what we see. In certain craft moves, your class can make up their own labels, but this is grammar, so give them the correct words to use like:

■ "The air crackling with heat" by itself would be a fragment because the auxiliary verb *was* is missing. "The air crackling with heat" is a dependent clause because it is dependent on the first part of the sentence for its meaning.

■ We could also cross out the conjunction *and* that now begins the third sentence. It adds a bit of emphasis to what Strider is doing. We would have to consider the content of the rest of the text to see if that *and* should stay or not. Before we changed the one sentence into three, that *and* was doing conventional grammar work as the *and* after the last series comma.

4. Now we *envision*. This is just one sentence we are looking at so I ask students to envision it in a finely tuned way. I ask, Can you see a narrative you might write starting out this way? Will a long, slow sentence with an inserted dependent clause fit with your content and the pace that you want for your reader? Note: This an explicit step toward a bigger picture of where they need to go—having an overall vision of what they want their piece to look like and sound like, big pacing and small pacing combined. We will get there. I am helping them construct that complex writerly envisioning strategy by working first specifically with just one sentence.

5. Finally, I push them to *apply*. All the inquiry in the world is no good without application, which is the final step to help our students really understand what they have noticed. It is the same as the notion that, as teachers, we have to write to understand the process. It's that personal experience that no amount of theorizing can give you. They must try writing this sentence structure. They can think of writing their sentence in the context of making a lead sentence to whatever narrative they are working on, or at the very least, they will try out this sentence construction in the context of an entry in their writers' notebooks. I always tell

them, "We are trying out this type of lead sentence because we need to learn possibilities for our writing. If you try it out and you decide not to use it in your draft, then you can always take it out or revise it." What I am asking them to do is called a try-it. But my students will correct me, "That's not a 'try-it'," they say, "that's a 'do-it', Mrs. Leograndis." They're right. It is.

Many students are able to write simple leads like "It was a warm summer day." And then they go on in their narrative with sentences of similar lengths and construction. Writing this complex sentence structure is difficult, so you will have to model it for them. Warning! Write yours up ahead of time, so you are sure not to get stuck. You could write up a three-sentence lead and then combine it. Whatever you think might work best for your group and grade level. Make sure that three-sentence lead is combinable by simply taking out the auxiliary verb from the middle sentence.

Here is my own writing example:

It was late one winter afternoon.
The weather was turning dark outside.
My sisters and I were setting up the Monopoly board.

Then I changed it to:

It was late one winter afternoon, the weather turning dark outside, when my sisters and I set up the Monopoly board.

I talk out loud through the choices I make, why *when* instead of *and* is a better word choice.

Before you excuse them to write on their own, listen in on turn-and-talks to make sure they have something in mind before you send them to their writers' notebooks. If they are really struggling, pull a small group together to work with.

Share struggles and successes in closure. Closure is always a great time for further learning and practicing articulation of process and purpose.

Looking at Student Writing

This is a difficult exercise at any grade level. But since it is a close study of one particular sentence structure, we see similar results. Iris, a fifth grader, wrote:

FIG. 8.4 *It was a warm summer evening, the windows opened wide, and a small breeze blew in my face.*

From Aoi, a third grader and language learner:

FIG. 8.5 *One early winter morning, when the sun was not up, my family was asleep in the Sand's hotel room.*

Day Two, Using Your Own Writing

For further meaning construction, students should be shown a contrasting example. A lead with a completely different pace from the *Before the Storm* lead. You want them to consider what sort of lead best suits the content of their own piece. Follow the five steps again, essentially doing the same lesson as before, but use, for example, the beginning few sentences of "Gimmetheball" instead.

Rewrite what you wrote in "Gimmetheball" form. This will sound ridiculous when it doesn't make sense for the content or the pacing. And that is what you want them to see.

Here's my Yolen-style lead sentence again:

It was late one winter afternoon, the weather turning dark outside, when my sisters and I set up the Monopoly board.

And my "Gimmetheball"-style lead written on the chart under my Yolen-style sentence:

What is she doing? The dice should be in *my* hands! There's only five hours left to play. Gimmethedice!

Have them turn and talk with a partner. What differences do they see? What do they notice in the pacing of the sentence structure as related to the content? What works and what doesn't and why? Then have them talk about what sort of lead would best match the content of the narrative they are considering writing. In any case, for practice, excuse them to rewrite their lead sentence from before into "Gimmetheball" form. This helps students to build understanding around the author's purpose and apply it in every choice they make. And it makes for a fun closure, with some silly sounding examples and some students deciding the "Gimmetheball" lead provides the best pacing for their content.

From this two-day lesson it is fairly simple to move on into completing a well-crafted beginning with purpose in pacing that matches content. You could choose to continue to study beginnings, past the lead sentence(s), in your classroom mentor texts to help your students turn their chosen leads into purposely paced beginnings.

Reading Workshop Support

Through informal discussion, continue to notice how sentence structure is purposeful to pace the writing in a way that supports the content. I also like to ask my students to specifically study the construction and content of lead sentences in their independent reading chapter books. One student found a perfect example you must see in the beginning of Lemony Snicket's *Series of Unfortunate Events, Book the Fourth* (2000).

Homework

Encourage students to continue experimenting with sentence length and structure for purpose in pacing. Discuss what they wrote as homework the next day, always encouraging articulation of process and purpose.

Related Reading

Grammatically Correct (1997), by Anne Stilman, pages 55-58, Basic Sentence Structure

LESSON 5: PUNCTUATION STUDY #1

Components: Content, Craft, and Conventions
Mentor Text Used: Your narrative study stack, be sure to spend the most time with familiar favorites, getting to know them better.
Previous Lessons/Background Knowledge Needed: Very little. Just a basic understanding of punctuation marks, that is, students can recognize and label a period, comma, exclamation point, and ellipses.

Lesson Introduction

Punctuation conventions can be taught so many different ways. But what is most effective for our students? I am sure my students have received instruction on the use of the period before they come to me. Why then, don't they all use them? And use them appropriately? I always get some students who use absolutely no periods at all, some that use them randomly after every oh, forty-five words or so, and some that place them around their pieces like so many bits of decoration.

A few years ago, while puzzling over this puzzle, I remembered that I had recently discovered inquiry is the one type of lesson that packs the most bang for the buck. Around the time of this revelation, Janet Angelillo's book, *A Fresh Approach to Teaching Punctuation* (2002), came out. I took a look and felt empowered to try out inquiry to teach punctuation. I dove in, or rather, had my students dive in for four days with great success. Students with no punctuation control suddenly were using periods correctly. Students with some sense of punctuation were using ending marks and ellipses with purpose, experimenting with meaning and nonconventional use as they found in our mentor texts.

Note please that I was also, as usual, fully using the reading connection. I was supporting our writing workshop punctuation work in reading workshop, especially assisting my language learners and struggling readers in small groups to hear those periods as we worked on their reading fluency.

You may have jumped here, to this lesson set, if you discovered your students generally have no ending punctuation. If you'd like, jump again and go directly to Janet Angelillo's wonderful book. I bring the pacing lens here to this quick punctuation study, but Janet has the complete book that you need.

This is a four-day lesson set because we take one punctuation mark per day: periods, commas, exclamation points, and ellipses. We don't do question marks, because I find students understand them—they may forget them sometimes, but they understand them.

The beautiful thing about this guided inquiry is even those students who appear to have control over their basic punctuation will find new levels of meaning and will begin to think more deeply about how they might use punctuation in the pacing work in their writing. And the students with no ending punctuation sense will gain control.

Using Mentor Texts

This is guided inquiry, but the only thing you are guiding is what punctuation mark you are looking for on which day. Let your students figure out why the marks are where they are. Let them figure out the author's purpose. If you have done the previous lessons in this chapter, including informal discussions in reading workshop around the author's purpose, then your students will amaze you with what they notice. In our discussions, I will get basic statements around the purpose of punctuation, things like "the period marks the end of the sentence—it's where you stop." But by now, if you've done the previous lessons in this chapter first, you will likely also see they are also looking for something more—for a deeper purpose.

I hear things like this about using periods to make short sentences:

To go fast, because the characters are in trouble.
To make it have suspense.

I hear things like this about comma use:

To slow the pace in a long sentence.
To slow down your breathing.

I hear things like this about using ellipses:

To add a long pause for suspense.
So the writer doesn't bore the reader by writing in all the words.

This is just a quick study to support the sentence length and sentence construction pacing work. But you will notice that you are also supporting students' growing habit of mind of reading like writers. This gift will help them to continually improve their writing, long after they leave your classroom.

The Exclamation Point

This is a punctuation mark that you would *think* students understand, like the question mark. But you might have a close look at your students' writing for *how* they are using this ending mark. What I often see in scoring stacks of student writing is misuse of the exclamation point. For instance:

Then we ate lunch!!!

or

We got to the parking lot!!!

There is no reason apparent to the reader for the three exclamation points. The sentence content is mundane, why is the writer shouting? If there is something terribly exciting about eating lunch or arriving at a parking lot and the writer chooses to deliver that excitement with only exclamation points, then the writer leaves the reader wondering, why did this writer decide not to give us all the details to show us why lunch was so exciting? Reader confused, pacing ruined.

If I see this problem in my students' writing I will address it in a quick direct-teaching, a what-not-to-do-and-why minilesson before I send them off to hunt for skilled writers' use of the exclamation point. I tell them there is no shortcut; in your writing you must provide details, the reader expects that, just like you do when you read. Remember that providing enough details is part of pacing your piece, so don't ask those exclamation marks to do the work that you should be doing. I address the whole group, not just the (hopefully) small group of offenders, because they all need to understand this point to support each other in peer conferences.

Of course, every day after the inquiry hunting and thinking and discussing, you allow plenty of time for writing, for applying. Have students go back into their writers' notebooks or drafts and do revision work toward using punctuation with purpose for pacing. Sharing in closure will bring more insights and meaning. Always encourage articulation of the reasons behind their application of punctuation marks in their revision or drafting work.

Reading Workshop Support

Tell students to watch for interesting uses of punctuation and add their findings to your chart. They will be excited to notice what writers do with punctuation and they'll bring it to you, unasked, for the rest of the year.

Homework Support

Each day, have them choose one punctuation mark and use it purposefully in a new notebook entry to help manage the pace of sentences in their writing. Or, they can go back and revise a previous notebook entry.

Related Readings

A Fresh Look at Punctuation (2002), by Janet Angelillo
Grammatically Correct (1997), by Anne Stilman, Part Three: Punctuation

Other Lesson Ideas in Basic Small Pacing

Here are some more ideas for lessons:

- Guided inquiry into purposeful use of the conjunction *and*. See Chapter 5 of this book and *Wondrous Words* (Ray 1999), page 171, "Artful Use of 'And'"
- Guided inquiry for small groups of language learners, attending to student's needs.
- Guided inquiry into purposeful sentence length and construction in literary informational writing.
- Although starting every sentence with *then* tends to naturally fall away after students internalize sentence length and structure variety, you may still see you need to do more work in starting sentences with purposeful variety.
- Instruction about time transitions.
- Any other lessons that support students' needs in terms of basic small pacing work based on what you see in ongoing assessment of their writing in relation to the standards or what you are passionate about teaching or what they have expressed interest in learning.

Advanced Big Pacing Lessons

We all get better at teaching writing over time and it shows in the ever-increasing improvements in our students' work. At the start of every school year I know I will have incoming students who are further along in their writing skills than the year before. Every year I know I will have to adjust my lessons to match my students' increasing level of abilities.

When I saw that students were coming to me with basic big pacing in place, I skipped to these more advanced lessons. I saw my students were no longer starting the school year writing "bed to bed" narratives. They came to me with a strong sense of writing around a single important idea. They had sequencing in place and a definite sense of beginning, middle, and end. What they needed was development of the depth and big pacing of story elements: setting, character, plot, and resolution.

ADVANCED BIG PACING LESSONS LIST

1. Story Arc
2. Snapshots
3. Thoughtshots and Shotthoughts
4. Planning a Story Arc Using The Big Three and The Big One
5. Threading the Point

LESSON 1: STORY ARC

Component: Content
Mentor Texts Used: *Owl Moon* (1987) by Jane Yolen, *My Rotten Redheaded Older Brother* (1998) by Patricia Polacco
Previous Lessons/Background Knowledge Needed: Knowledge of beginning, middle, and end. Some familiarity with story elements—setting, character, plot, and resolution—from reading workshop work.

Lesson Introduction

It was a few years ago when I originally started using the concept of story arc to help my students pace their pieces. At that time, I used the arc as a visual to teach them to hold the pace through to the end (see Chapter 7, List Strategy). We plotted out the events in stories, just thinking of the simple definition of a narrative: events that move through time.

Then I started to understand I could use story arcs to help students see how much time a writer takes to tell not just the beginning, middle, and end but also how much time is spent in which story element. It's big pacing management either way. The story arc can be used to scaffold understanding narrative writing: there are story elements in your beginning, middle, and end. The story arc is a scaffold to that deeper understanding: when you write narrative, you're not just selecting and sequencing relevant events and details, you are crafting a *story*. Stories have story elements and how long you stay in each element sets the big pacing. The pacing of expected story elements must be attended to with purpose, whether it's personal narrative or fiction.

A Few Considerations

Plot may not always look like much of a plot in personal narrative. There may not be a developed conflict and resolution, or problem or solution. A student may simply be writing a carefully crafted sequence of events about a simple and short bit of time, where there really is no obvious turning point or conflict or goal or even a problem—they are writing a small moment narrative.

By the time in the year I get to working in story arc to pace story elements we have left the small moment study and are working on topics with a bit more significance to the student writer; students are now writing "significant event" narratives or memoirs. We will have immersed ourselves in significant event or memoir writing and we will have noticed the depth of the narratives we study. Students will be choosing topics that will easily lend themselves to work in story elements. They will be choosing a topic where they write about a change in their thinking (like *Thundercake*) or a relationship (like *My Rotten Redheaded Older Brother*) or about a difficult or exhilarating "first time" event (like *White Water*). They will be choosing a topic where there will be a problem, a goal, a struggle, a conflict, a turning point. In other words, a plot. And a plot requires the support of setting and developed characters.

Before this lesson, build familiarity with story elements in your reading workshop and informally discuss story elements while in the immersion work for your significant event or memoir unit. Show them in your read-alouds that the same story elements are there whether the story is in first or third person, personal narrative or fiction, and with people or mice as characters.

This story arc lesson is a foundational lesson. You might want to do it in your reading workshop because there won't be any actual writing. Or you could do pieces of it over a few days in your writing workshop, while still having writing time. I do the latter. Big concepts are always better broken up over a few days. New learning takes time to process, and students will need lots of revisiting this concept.

While this lesson scaffolds understanding of story elements, later, in your writing workshop, you will work with specific strategies writers use to craft story elements, for instance: snapshots for setting, thoughtshots for character development, exploded moment for the turning point of the story. This lesson is just to have a close look, a scaffolded look at the elements first.

A story arc is a concept you can use to help students understand that they need to carefully develop their stories. I use it as a visual aide, to show the development of a story on paper—the rise and fall of action. I have seen other representational drawings of the rise and fall of action in a story, with a line rising to a pointy peak representing the turning point or climax, then falling abruptly back down to represent resolution. I prefer to use just one visual to chart the elements in a story. I don't want to take the time and potentially confuse my students or myself with different visuals for different stories. And since it is a rare story that moves along on such a perfectly straight incline then climaxes in such a precisely pointy way, I prefer to use just a simple arc when talking about any narrative. I believe the arc gives a kinder nod to the complexities of storytelling.

Using Mentor Texts

I like keeping a simple, small chart, just a list of the story elements on my wall for students to use as a quick reference. The chart is not cluttered with a lot of writing and explanations. It's just there for students to learn the words and cue our thinking. I see students refer to this chart frequently, so it stays up all year.

I had the word *conclusion* listed instead of *resolution* on the chart for quite a while. *Resolution* is a better word for a plot with a definite conflict, but *resolution* can also broadly mean how the story is wrapped up, even if there was no real conflict. *Conclusion* sounds more formal to me, and more suitable for expository text.

After spending time discussing the story elements in your reading workshop, you now begin to build the bridge toward understanding the writing side of the coin.

Guided Inquiry

Introduce the big idea: *Writers control the big pacing in their narratives by deciding how much time to spend in each story element.*

Before this lesson, in your initial immersion into your study stacks of significant event, personal narrative, or memoir, you narrowed down the stack to a few classroom favorites that you and your students decided you would study more deeply. From those familiar few, choose two contrasting examples, two that are different in pacing, one like *Owl Moon,* which is soft and slow and spends a lot of time in the setting element, and another like *My Rotten Redheaded Older Brother,* which is just a bit faster and spends more obvious time in the element of character development.

Distribute typed-up text-boxed copies (temporary classroom use only, see page 165) of your two choices to your students and decide, based on your students' needs and ability to handle this learning, whether you should:

■ Gather them in your meeting area so you can guide their understanding.
■ Let them go off in groups or pairs and do the work on their own.
■ A combination of the two—send off some, gather others.

In any case, you will want them each to take a pencil and jot on the margin of the typed text boxes which story elements they notice on that page.

When you gather as a whole class again to discuss findings, you may have the tricky job of showing them that while it may appear that so many pages contain just setting in *Owl Moon*, there is also subtle character development as we are given little hints as to the child and father's personalities. You may have to show them when there is action that is moving the plot, the simple looking-for-an-owl plot, and when it's just setting. You may even be able to guide them to the big learning that setting supports plot.

After you decide on what is setting, character development, plot, and resolution, draw a simple arc shape on chart paper, and have students help you plot out—using the first initial for each story element, each in different colored marker—the arc of story elements across *Owl Moon*.

On the second day of the lesson, do the same procedure as the first day but this time with your second mentor text choice.

As you and your students compare the marked difference of how many S's and C's and P's and R's you have on each arc, record their noticings and start asking questions like:

■ Why is there more time spent in setting in one book, and not the other?
■ What does this organization of the elements do for the big pacing? And how does that pacing choice the writer made support content?
■ Have we seen any other books like these? With similar time spent in similar elements and was the pacing the same?

On the third day, you could give students a chance at independent practice and have partners choose one familiar book from your study stack. Tell them to draw their own arc and chart the story elements of the familiar book on the arc. Review how each element gets its own color; it'll be easier to see differences and similarities. They should be able to do this on their own now, after your two days of scaffolding with guided practice.

If you have students do their own arcs on a half sheet of chart paper, you can pin them up around the room and have a gallery walk, with students sharing what they found out. Talk about the author's purpose and why writers spend a long time or a short time in each element. Compare the arcs to each other. You will probably need to nudge and guide their thinking. Find examples that contrast the most. It's easier to talk about a writer's purpose when you have contrasting examples. Tie your talk back to the river metaphor, what kinds of a river rides have these writers crafted for their reader? Tie it back to talk about big pacing, about how the reader will breathe differently with different books because of how the writer controls the pace of the story arc by deciding how much time to spend in each story element. That's the point you are trying to make in this foundational lesson.

One example would be, "Gimmetheball" by Charles R. Smith, which would have an arc with very little time spent on setting, and a lot on character development (through action and internal monologue). The resolution is quite brief. The writer's purpose? He has crafted an intense scene that is paced very quickly through the eyes and mind of just this one character. We don't know what the setting is, other than a basketball court, and we don't need to. A long time spent in describing the setting—the heat, the black asphalt, the chain link fence, or maybe the squeak of sneakers on a polished wood gymnasium floor—is content that would slow the pace of the story that Smith wants to tell. In your discussions of the author's purpose, help your students see the deliberate choices a writer makes.

In *My Rotten Redheaded Older Brother* Patricia Polacco spends a nearly even amount of time in each of the story elements, with a bit more in character development, making for a smooth, evenly paced story appropriate to the author's purpose and content of the reflection back in time about her relationship with her brother and how it changed. And in *Owl Moon,* Jane Yolen spends a lot of time in the setting story element, slowing the pace of this gentle, quiet story throughout.

You want your students to be aware of the choices they make as writers. They need to see they can control the pace of their narratives and the reader expects them to have control. As the writer, they make the choices about how long to spend in which story element. They need to be able to articulate the purpose behind their choices like, "I decided to spend no time in setting because I want to craft a fast piece like 'Gimmetheball.'" "I decided to spend a long time in setting at the beginning of my piece because I want to set up a slow and thoughtful pace like in *Owl Moon*." Their choices and purpose should match and support the content of their pieces. The big pacing strategies are purposeful choices that a writer makes to support the content of their piece. Once students understand this, then you are ready to teach strategies to support your student writers' choices.

LESSON 2: SNAPSHOTS

Component: Content
Mentor Texts Used: Study stack of favorite narrative picture books
Previous Lessons/Background Knowledge Needed: Story Arc

Lesson Introduction

Snapshots and *thoughtshots* are from Barry Lane's book *After the End,* along with Explode the Moment discussed in Chapter 7. They are excellent pacing tools. Snapshots help to develop the story elements of settings and character. Thoughtshots help to develop character. He has these important strategies for student writers and much more in his wonderful book and I encourage you to get a copy or reread the one you have.

Lane presents his exercises primarily as revision strategies. But as he argues in his book, revision occurs throughout the writing process. I have used his snapshots, thoughtshots, and exploded moments as revision lessons and they are powerful. One year, I decided to try something different with my group of third grade writers. I decided to try teaching snapshots, exploded moments, and thoughtshots first, as strategies to try out in their notebooks prior to drafting. We worked on understanding where these pieces might fit in the pacing of an entire narrative, so when they did start on drafts, they had already developed the skills and knowledge needed to use these strategies with purpose. I thought it went fairly well. When we were finished learning about and practicing the strategies, I read the strongest first drafts I had ever seen.

While on yard duty one day, I was discussing my choice—to teach the strategies before drafting—with Madeleine, a student of mine, new to the school and to writing workshop. I was so impressed with her thoughtfulness and articulation. She said:

> If you learn it before you draft, then you can experiment with it in your writers' notebook and once you understand it you can put it in your piece.
>
> If you draft first you have to start all over again and you would say, "But I already have my draft, why couldn't we have learned this before?"

Based on her affirmation, and the success I saw in my class, I plan to continue to teach these strategies first, prior to drafting a first significant event or personal narrative.

When you do foundational work in story elements and story arc, students will have strategies to practice and develop when crafting their narratives, strategies to help them develop their different story elements. You are going to start first, in this lesson, with a craft strategy called the snapshot. I always show my students where I get my ideas from, or what all I have used to synthesize new ideas. It is important for us to model for our students that we are lifelong learners. I show them Barry Lane's book and I talk with them about how it is one of many books I use to help me be a better teacher. I tell them Lane developed the concept called *snapshots* to help writers "to write in sharp physical detail" (1993, 32).

I talk with them about how snapshots, or writing with attention to physical detail, serve to slow the pace while developing a setting or a character, or both. The snapshot slows the pace because the action stops and the writer gives the reader a chance to look around the setting or to closely study a character. Lane also explains that the writer's camera is magic. I show them how Lane uses a snapshot from Laura Ingalls Wilder's *Little House in the Big Woods* (1971), which shows a snapshot that includes a little movement and sound with Ma kissing the kids good night, tucking the covers, and sewing by lamplight with clicking and swishing of the needle and thread.

Then I can see I am starting to loose my students with the magic camera idea until I ask them to consider the magic photographs in the Harry Potter movies. There is no story action, no plot happening, it is just a photo in a newspaper or in a frame. The characters are stuck there, but they might be smiling and waving at you. Once my students have that schema retrieved, it's not too far of a stretch to ask them to consider adding sounds and smells to their snapshots.

Using a Mentor Text

I have shown them the Laura Ingalls Wilder snapshot from Lane's book, we've discussed the Harry Potter photos. Now comes the hard part: finding snapshots from our own mentor texts.

First I review: A snapshot gives your reader a strong sense of place. A snapshot pulls your reader into your story—he or she can visualize being there because you have given so many precise physical details. Then again I refer them to the chart "Good Writing Has Detail" to help them understand (see Figure 7–6 on page 93). Then, if I have decided on a direct teaching lesson, I will have preselected a snapshot from one of our favorite narratives and written it on a chart.

Depending on how much scaffolding students need, choose one of these ways to present the lesson:

- Direct teaching. Discuss your example on the chart, point out all the details used. Or write your own example on a chart and next to that, write a plain version of your snapshot as a nonexample. If your students are drafting or revising a piece have them envision where they might use a snapshot in their own writing, where do they want to slow the pace way down, to have their reader freeze in the story and have a look around? Then ask them to turn and talk with a partner to help their thinking, and send them off to write their own snapshot. If they are not drafting or revising, have them practice the strategy in their writers' notebooks.
- Guided Inquiry. Do this if you are not comfortable finding a snapshot or writing your own example. After studying the Laura Ingalls Wilder snapshot from Lane's book, have your students hunt for snapshots from your study stacks or in preselected familiar text that you have passed out. Ask them to notice what makes it a snapshot, ask questions as to purpose for the pacing in the particular part of the story, and finally help them help themselves envision—by turning and talking with a partner—about where a snapshot might go in their own pieces Then send them off to apply it to their writing or to practice constructing snapshots in their notebooks.

STRATEGIES FOR WRITING A SNAPSHOT

If your students can learn what a snapshot is by studying mentor texts, wonderful. I always find mine need extra help:

- **The Freeze.** Have students stand, imagine themselves in their story, close their eyes and freeze. Tell them to look around in the story, but don't move, stay frozen in that one spot and see and hear and smell all that they can. Now write.
- **Gift Questions.** You can model this strategy by demonstrating it with a student in front of the whole class, a fish bowl model. The student reads his or her writing to

you and asks for help developing his or her snapshot. As they read the part they want help developing, you write a list of questions focused on getting more details about what things looked like, sounded like, and smelled like. As the student writer reads, model holding up your hand or saying stop to give yourself time to write down your questions. Then model giving the questions as a gift from a reader to help a writer.

■ **The Zoom-in.** Going with the camera idea: students draw a picture of their snapshot, write about it, zoom-in on one part of it, draw it bigger with more detail, write more, and again zoom-in on a part of the second drawing, draw it bigger with more detail, write more.

Looking at Student Writing

I find the snapshot concept one of the most difficult for my students to understand. They do eventually get it, at varying levels. And all along they talk like they get it. But they are young and working to get control over their writing. Even after practicing the freezing strategy I find it's difficult for some of them to stop the action in their narratives and write a snapshot with "sharp physical detail" to give the reader a sense of place, or a sense of a character. For instance, after working with the students in snapshots through direct teaching and guided inquiry and work in their writers' notebooks, I had a conference with Vanessa while she was working on a draft. She was having a lot of trouble understanding how she could freeze in one spot in her story and look around:

Denise: How's it going? What are you working on today?

Vanessa: I want to work on my snapshot.

Denise: Your snapshot. Great. Show me where you want to have your snapshot.

Vanessa: (*points*)

Denise: Right here? Where are you in your story right here?

Vanessa: I am at Yosemite.

Denise: Where in Yosemite?

Vanessa: I am chasing my brother.

Denise: No, not the action in your story, the place in your story, where are you?

Vanessa: I am on a big rock, then I jump down and chase my brother.

Denise: Wait, not the action, get back on the rock, before you chase your brother, freeze, close your eyes and stay there, stay on the rock. What do you feel?

Vanessa: The rock is hot.

Denise: What do you see?

Vanessa: Trees, a river . . .

Denise: What do you hear?

Vanessa: A waterfall.

Denise: Can you see it, or do you have to turn your head?

Vanessa: It's behind me.

Denise: Vanessa, when writers are working to write a snapshot about a place where they have been, one strategy is to go there in their minds, freeze themselves in the spot they want to remember and then very carefully notice what is around them and then describe what they notice. Can you go back to that rock and stay on that rock and write about what is around you?

Vanessa: Yes.

Denise: How are you going to do that?

Vanessa: I'll stay on the rock and write about what is around me.

Denise: Good job, I look forward to reading your snapshot.

I knew from an earlier conversation that Vanessa was one of many students who had decided to have a slow moment followed by a sudden change in pace, just like we had noticed in one of our favorite mentor texts, *White Water.* The where and why of her snapshot had already been decided, and I didn't discuss it with her again in this conference. Maybe I should have to help her focus on that one spot on the rock because the difficulty for her was stopping her action so she could develop the snapshot itself. Students get excited about telling their stories, the action. They need to learn they are not *telling* a story, they are *crafting* a story and they need to be diligent about the pacing of their story elements. After our conference Vanessa stayed on the rock and wrote her snapshot (see Figure 9–1). Brief but beautiful.

> The next day there wasn't a cloud in the sky as I sat there on a rock looking at the littel fish trying to go the other way. My Mom said be quiet hear the river.

FIG. 9.1 *The next day there wasn't a cloud in the sky as I sat there on a rock looking at the little fish trying to go the other way. My mom said be quiet and hear the river.*

Helping our students control the pace of their writing is difficult. They'll eventually get it, with practice and guidance and inquiry and a continual return to the reading connection.

Reading Workshop Support

You can continue to support students' learning by asking them to listen for snapshots in your read-alouds, then have them discuss what the snapshot does for the reader, the reader's breathing, the pace.

Homework Support

Have them freeze in real time—take their writers' notebooks outside or inside their home and practice writing snapshots. Share process and articulate purpose the next day, as in where might you use a snapshot like this and what would it do for your story?

Related Readings

how's it going? (2000), by Carl Anderson, for excellent reading on improving your conferring and your minilessons

After the End (1993), by Barry Lane, page 32

Revisor's Tool Box (1999), by Barry Lane, pages 74–89 and 245–246

Teaching the Qualities of Writing (2004), by Joann Portalupi and Ralph Fletcher, page D-31
"Use Details to Alter the Pace of Time"

LESSON 3: THOUGHTSHOTS AND SHOTTHOUGHTS

Components: Content and Craft

Mentor Texts Used: *White Water* (2001) by Jonathan and Aaron London, *Fishing Sunday* (1996) by Tony Johnston

Previous Lessons/Background Knowledge Needed: Story Arc

Lesson Introduction

There are many, many ways to develop character: through physical descriptions, through actions and dialogue. But internal monologue lets you see inside the character's mind, allowing the reader to hear a character's thoughts, it's a character development tool that writers readily employ because it works so well. Barry Lane calls them *thoughtshots*. One year, when my students were searching through study stacks, they identified a particular kind of internal monologue they labeled the *shotthought*. We'll look at thoughtshots first.

Using Mentor Texts

Depending on your students, you could explain a thoughtshot and send them to do guided inquiry through your study stacks, looking for places where the reader can hear the thoughts of a character, then gather and discuss your findings. But I find my students have trouble, initially, distinguishing dialogue from internal monologue. I find I need to do some explicit teaching to show them the difference, therefore, I prefer to do direct teaching for this lesson.

I have this bit of dialogue, from *White Water*, copied onto an overhead or chart paper:

> Dad told me again how much fun white water rafting was. "And by the end," he said, "you'll learn to read the river—which way looks safer, which way is more dangerous."
>
> I was quiet, thinking about how scary it would be. Here the river was flat, but what did it become around those huge rock walls?

Below this example, I rewrite the thoughtshot into dialogue:

> I was quiet, I was thinking. Then I said to my dad, "I think it will be scary. The river is flat here, dad, but will happen when we go around those huge rock walls?"

Things to point out:

- In the rewrite, the character is thinking, but out loud. That makes it dialogue, not internal monologue.
- The pacing is slowed as the writer gives us a moment to hear the character's thoughts. This thoughtshot starts with "I was quiet, thinking about . . ." but thoughtshots can start other ways, such as with "I wondered. . . ," I couldn't believe. . . ," "I was thinking. . . ," or "I thought to myself. . . . "

Have students take some time to look in their writers' notebooks or drafts, to look for parts where they could slow the pace with some character development, what kind of thoughtshot they could write and then have them think out their idea with a turn-and-talk.

Discuss struggles and successes in closure. And since this was a quick, direct lesson, be sure to do supporting work in your reading workshop and with a homework try-it.

Looking at Student Writing

Even though you are working with this big pacing strategy—thoughtshots—you will still be discussing small pacing strategies because the small supports the big. After students begin to put thoughtshots in their pieces, be on the lookout for one with clunking small pacing, which you could use as a whole-class example on an overhead when doing some revision work. Or write up your own thoughtshot with poor small pacing to use as an example. In this lesson you aren't teaching any one specific strategy to smooth the small pacing because there are infinite strategies to help a piece sound better. You are drawing attention to clunking pacing and you are asking the class to help you figure out what *sounds* better. If you have tuned their ears through the reading connection, they will be able to come up with a variety of ways to smooth out a piece of writing.

After doing some whole-class small pacing work, Varun assessed his own thoughtshot (Figure 9–2), noticed it needed revision work to read smoothly, and worked with his writing partner and in a response group until he was happy with his revised thoughtshot (see Figure 9–3).

I was walking toward the green roller coaster, I was wondering, I decided against it. As we approached the green roller coaster, I shuddered. I was thinking I would fall off the roller coaster.

FIG. 9.2

We saw a green roller coaster.

My dad asked me, "Want to go on that ride?"

In my mind I said no but I said yes to my dad. I shuddered as we approached the roller coaster.

> We saw a green roller coaster.
>
> My dad asked me, "Want to go on that ride?"
>
> In my mind I said no but I said yes to my dad. I shuddered as we approached the roller coaster.

FIG. 9.3

Varun used a number of small pacing strategies to make this thoughtshot effective. He put "We saw a green roller coaster" in its own paragraph for emphasis and suspense. He added dialogue to further set up the thoughtshot. He changed "As we approached the green roller coaster, I shuddered" to "I shuddered as we approached the green roller coaster." It sounds better, has better rhythm. Varun was learning how to revise his writing so it would have the sound of well-crafted, well-paced writing. Yes, I drew his attention through the whole-class lesson to small pacing problems, but he did the work himself of looking for problems in his own piece. And then he had to figure out what would make it *sound* better. On his own. Because I never showed him one exact strategy to smooth the small pacing in his particular thoughtshot, he was showing the results of the reading connection where sound of well-crafted, well-paced language trickles down into our students' writing.

The Shotthought

When my students were looking through *Fishing Sunday* they discovered a kind of internal monologue where the main character is imagining what other characters are thinking. In this example, a Japanese boy is very embarrassed to be going fishing with his grandfather. And although all the people on the fishing boat like his grandfather, the boy doesn't see things that way. The author never uses the word *embarrassed*, instead, she shows the reader through this "shotthought," in the author's italics:

> I know what their smiles mean. *Here comes that old Japanese fool. The only English he knows is "Fishing Sunday." And he fishes with bones.*

It goes on, the boy imaging disparaging comments about his grandfather's feet. This is a powerful character development tool that can also be used to move the plot forward. The boy changes his mind about his grandfather at the end of the story through some well-crafted scenes rich in character description.

My students take to this strategy like they take to the What-If Strategy (discussed in Chapter 10). Every year, I teach it directly and ask the new group to give it their own term. Some groups stick to shotthought. I have also had mind-control thoughtshot and last year, they named it the thinking-what-they're-thinking thoughtshot.

Looking at Student Writing

Students learn to use the shotthought as a way to slow their pace and develop character. I have typically seen a shotthought used as a show not tell character development tool, usually to show the reader how nervous the student was at a point in their personal narratives. Figure 9-4 is an example from Aaron's "The Story of My First Horseback Ride."

A horse was snorting, I Know what that snorting means—what a little boy, thinks he can hold on to me, he's just going to fall off on that last hill. He's really, really, really, crazy.

FIG. 9.4

A horse was snorting. I knew what that snorting meant—what a little boy, thinks he can hold on to me, he's just going to fall off on that last hill. He's really, really, really crazy.

Reading Workshop Support

Ask students to be on the lookout for thoughtshots and shotthoughts in their reading so you can add the source to a list on a chart for future reference. Discuss the author's purpose and the effect on pacing.

Homework Support

You can assign students to go back in their writers' notebook entries, find a narrative type entry and revise it, adding a thoughtshot. Next day, discuss how the thoughtshot affects the pace of the entry.

Related Readings

After the End, by Barry Lane, page 44, "Climbing the Mountain: Thoughtshots"

LESSON 4: PLANNING A STORY ARC USING THE "BIG 3" AND THE "BIG 1"

Component: Content

Mentor Texts Used: *White Water* (2001) by Jonathan and Aaron London, *My Rotten Redheaded Older Brother* (1998) by Patricia Polacco

Previous Lessons/Background Knowledge Needed: Students need to have a strong sense of beginning, middle, and end. Previous lessons in snapshots, thoughtshots, exploded moments, and time compression are needed.

Lesson Introduction

This lesson is all about planning the rise and fall of action in a story, or you can call it the plot development, or the rising action to the climax or some call it the buildup to the turning point followed by resolution. Call it what you want, it's about big pacing. It's about showing your students that writers control the flow and balance of their stories, spending the right amount of time on the buildup, the right amount of time on the big moment, and the right amount of time on the resolution. Writers take the reader over the arc of their story, from beginning, middle, to end. This is a planning strategy lesson to help students manage the arc of their narratives.

The Big 3: Using a Mentor Text

Draw an arc on your chart paper. Show the students a familiar book that takes the reader through a set of three events. I use *White Water.* Together, plot the story—using strategies that your students have in place, snapshots, thoughtshots, exploded moments, time compression—over the arc on the chart paper. Use symbols that you and your students have agreed upon. For instance, in *White Water*, the story arc you co-create might look like Figure 9–5.

The authors have, of course, managed the time compression well (see previous time compression lesson, Chapter 7, Lesson 2 on page 88). And they have given the reader slow-downs in the pacing with the balance of lovely snapshots. (See previous snapshot lesson, this chapter, Lesson 2 on page 131.) But look at how they deliberately chose to explode three, exactly three, white water events, each more intense than the last, so the last one is the scariest, and most exploded of all. I ask my students to consider using the "Big 3" to balance the pacing in their stories. And I also ask them to consider "fictionalizing the truth"—do they have to write the events in the order they actually happened? I ask them, Do you think, when Jonathan London and his son were on this river adventure in real life, that the scariest set of rapids actually, conveniently for his later storywriting, occurred last? There is thought on their faces and silence at first, then Ah ha! My students say, as the construction of the meaning of what it is to be a writer gets a little clearer. They are now thinking, I can mess with this thing that I am writing about that happened to me—the truth is I was scared the first time I went rock climbing, and through several attempts at climbing at varying levels of intensity, I finally got over my fear, but I can rearrange the actual events to pace my story well and make my meaning most effective for my reader. Ah ha!

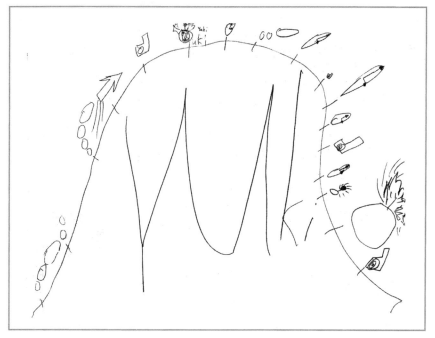

FIG. 9.5

FIG. 9.6

I love to see their faces when this reality dawns on them—fictionalizing truth. I know then I am beginning to get a room full of writers, students with a real sense of audience. And it's the beginning of understanding how to write good fiction—it's not about the aliens, it's about constructing story.

Looking at Writing

Yuki was writing about a rock climbing day with his dad and friends. He drew out his story plan over an arc, choosing the three most intense climbing events of the day out of seven. He time compressed four, and rearranged the three, so the most intense was last. He was acting as a writer. He was thinking of audience. He deliberately rearranged the truth in order to pace his story well. (See Figure 9–6.)

I noticed students who have a particularly difficult time planning and controlling their pieces, including students with sequencing processing difficulties, use the story arc with success, gaining control over their story lines. I have also noticed students using the story arcs to help plan for a narrative prompt. Some draw it out, some do it in their heads before they begin to write.

The Big 1

I remember, after showing the class The Big 3, some of my students thoughtfully came to me to say that a rising set of three events would not work for their piece. They said there was one big moment and that was it. We jokingly called it The Big 1 and the name stuck. You could support these students with inquiry work into what the Big 1 looks like on a story arc. Guide them to understand that the choices they make in the amount of snapshots, thoughtshots, time compression, and the length of their exploded moments all indicate how their big pacing will unfold.

Reading Workshop Support

Have students watch for The Big 3 in larger stories, like the independent chapter books they are reading. It's often there as it's a natural way to balance a story—the hero tries three times at something before succeeding, for example.

Homework Support

Have students revisit a narrative idea in their writers' notebooks and consider rearranging main events and time compressing some events to control the story for The Big 3. Have them draw their plan on a story arc.

Related Readings

There may be something out there, written for teachers, on story arcs, but I haven't run across it yet. There's a bit on the Net.

LESSON 5: THREADING THE POINT

Component: Content
Mentor Texts Used: NCEE Third Grade "At Standard" Narrative, "When My Puppies Ran Away," or *Thundercake* by Patricia Polacco
Previous Lessons/Background Knowledge Needed: Basic understanding of story elements: beginning, middle, and end

Lesson Introduction

Students need to see what the standards look like in student writing for their grade level. You could use grade-level anchor papers now and then for mentor texts. Or use previous writing you have saved over the years of fine student work.

Using a Mentor Text

"When My Puppies Ran Away" is a beautifully paced piece of student writing. It flows. Until the end. Then you wish you could have just one conference back in time with this child, just one, to guide that smooth pace all the way through. It's a wonderful paper to show your students how to thread the point through the story and just as importantly, how the point is lost at the end. If you don't have access to this piece of writing, look for a piece of student writing where the point is obviously threaded throughout the piece. Make copies of "When My Puppies Ran Away" or another student paper and pass them out to all students.

If you would rather not use student writing, study one of your classroom touchstones for the threaded point. *Thundercake* is a good choice because the point—the little girl is scared— is so obviously threaded. Print up a text-boxed copy (see page 165) of the book you have chosen and pass one out to everyone. Every one will need their own copy.

Either with your student writing sample or *Thundercake* or the like, have your students go through and circle every place that the point of the story comes up. In "My Puppies Ran Away," they will be circling all the references to worrying, and then to crying. In *Thundercake*, every mention of being scared, which changes to brave.

Now get a long piece of black construction paper, a hole punch, and a piece of white yarn. After you and your class are in agreement as to what is the threaded point and where the point appears, reread the piece, and whenever the point of the story comes up, punch a hole in the black paper, then leave a space. Do the same for the next reference— hole, space, and so on— down the length of the black paper. Now take your yarn and reread the whole story again, threading "the point" with your yarn as you go. You will make your point concretely and visually. At the end of the puppies piece, when the thread is lost in the too-quick ending, be sure to leave some dangling yarn, so the students can see the pacing was lost and therefore the writer lost the reader.

Reading Workshop Support

Discussions about the author's message and point will support this learning. During your whole-class reading time, have students find sentences and phrases that support the author's point. Guide them to notice that the sentences and phrases thread through the story.

Homework Support

Have them revisit one of their narratives in their writers' notebooks and decide what the point was and see if their point was threaded. If not, they should revise.

Related Reading

Teaching the Qualities of Writing (2004) by JoAnn Portalupi and Ralph Fletcher, page D-4, "Use a Recurring Detail"

Other Lesson Ideas in Advanced Big Pacing

- Talk more about text structure. It's all about big pacing. Alphabet books and see-saw texts, story-within-a-story, and conversation texts each have their own flow, balance, and rhythm created by the structure. Excellent reading and lesson ideas are found in Ray's *Wondrous Words*, Chapter 7.
- Add more work in developing character with purpose toward pacing.
- Work in transitions, segues, between fast- and slowly paced parts so the pacing stays smooth.
- Any other lessons that will support students' needs based on what you see in ongoing assessment of their writing in relation to the standards or what you are passionate about teaching or what they have expressed interest in learning.

Advanced Small Pacing Lessons

I will often use more advanced small pacing lessons in a revision unit, where we are working to fine-tune a piece of writing that already has big pacing and basic small pacing under control.

Other years I have used some of these lessons in a basic study, generally the first three, but it depends on my class. Again, this is a thinking curriculum, you decide what your students would benefit from most and in what order.

As in all the lesson chapters, this is not a definitive list by any means. There are countless ways that writers craft small pacing. These are just a start for you and your students. As your class does the inquiry work of reading like a writer, you will find other interesting craft moves that you can use to improve the level of the flow, the balance, the rhythm in your students' writing.

SLIGHTLY ADVANCED TO MORE ADVANCED SMALL PACING LESSONS LIST

1. The Magic Three
2. The What-If Strategy
3. Pacing in Paragraphing
4. Punctuation Study #2
5. Vivid Verbs and Pacing

LESSON 1: THE MAGIC THREE

Component: Craft
Mentor Texts Used: *Going North* (2004) by Janice N. Harrington, *Fishing in the Air* (2000) by Sharon Creech, *The Relatives Came* (1993) by Cynthia Rylant, *Shortcut* (1992) by Donald Crews, *Beekeepers* (1998) by Linda Oatman High, and most any favorite narrative you have
Previous Lessons/Background Knowledge Needed: Basic understanding of sentence structure

Lesson Introduction

Refer back to Chapter 4 where we looked at the phenomenon of things in writing occurring in sets of three. My students call it the Magic Three. They love to spot threes and they love to use them in their writing. It's a literary way with words that students can easily manage to add rhythm to their small pacing.

Using Mentor Texts

You can simply pass around study stacks of narrative picture books and have students work with a partner. It's a fun inquiry project. Students will find lots of magic threes because they're everywhere. Almost in every book you will have. Some students will recognize things in threes in the simplest form, "We went faster, faster, faster." Some will spot more complicated forms of the magic three like this short, short, long in Sharon Creech's *Fishing in the Air:*

> "When I was a boy," my father said, "I caught the air, I caught the breeze, and I took them home with me."

After noticing and gathering examples of magic threes, you will want to ask questions. What does this magic three do for the pacing in the writing? Does it slow it down, or speed it up, or smooth it out? As a reader, what do the threes do to my breathing? How do threes work with the content of the piece? Are there places in writing where they fit and places were they don't sound right? Do different magic threes, from simple to more complex, have different purposes? When we look at magic threes in use across different texts, do we see the same purposes?

We label the simple ones, we label the short, short, longs and the others that we find and we see if we can identify any difference in the purposes. Whatever you and your students come up with is correct as long as it makes sense. Be sure to label whatever you identify so you can talk about it, in the language of your classroom, at any time.

After noticing, asking questions, and labeling, the next step is to ask your students to envision using the magic threes in their own writing. You've discussed purposes so now they consider where in their writing is there a place where a similar purpose will work?

Final learning will come with purposeful application. Send your students to their drafts or writers' notebooks to apply. Be sure to have them articulate purpose in closure.

Looking at Student Writing

Adding magic threes will improve the sound of your students' writing, adding a pleasing complexity to the rhythm in the structure of their sentences. Figure 10–1 is from Aaron's first draft of his memoir, "The Story of My First Horseback Ride." Figure 10–2 shows Aaron's second draft with magic three revision.

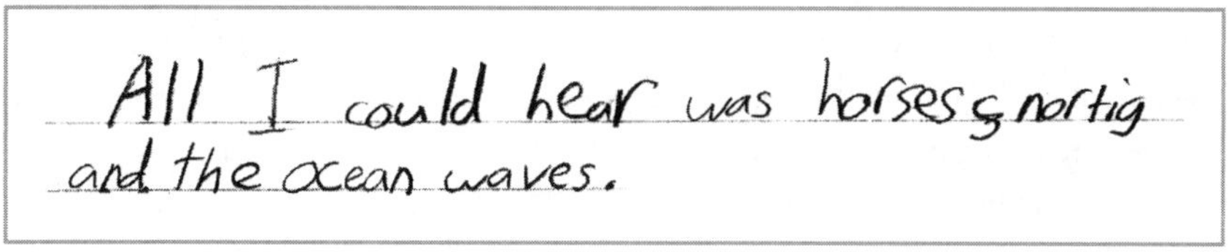

> *All I could hear was horses snorting and the ocean waves.*

FIG. 10.1 *All I could hear was horses snorting and the ocean waves.*

From Aaron's second draft with magic three revision:

> *All I could here were horses snorting, the ocean waves, and people talking.*

FIG. 10.2 *All I could hear were horses snorting, the ocean waves, and people talking.*

Have you ever had a student who writes some beautiful craft in a first or second draft, and by the time he or she has finished the piece, the craft has been revised away? Or just cut it out altogether? Maddening. If our students don't recognize the sound of well-crafted writing, if they can't label craft moves and articulate purpose, then they can't produce well-crafted writing. Any accidentally produced craft is in danger.

Students will quickly pick up the sound of magic threes, put them in their writing and leave them there, liking what they do for their small pacing, liking the sound, liking the craft. I found this one, shown in Figure 10–3, untouched, in all four of Gina's drafts of her memoir "The Jungle" even though lots of revision work was going on all around it.

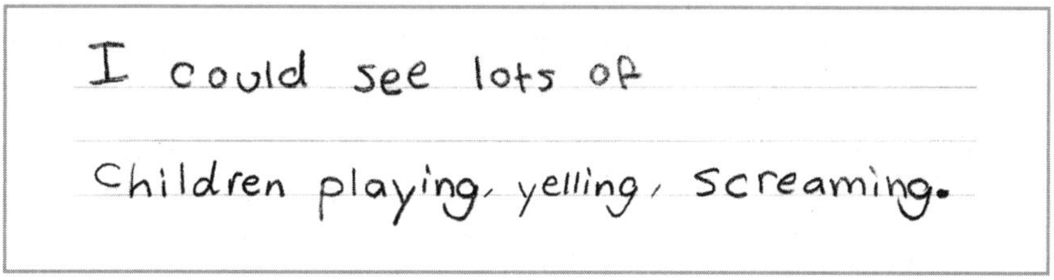

> *I could see lots of children playing, yelling, screaming.*

FIG. 10.3 *I could see lots of children playing, yelling, screaming.*

Reading Workshop Support

Once you open the door to the magic threes your students will begin to see them in their independent reading. For the reading workshop time that follows the magic three lesson, I ask them to put sticky notes on pages with magic threes they notice and we share them in closure, always articulating the author's purpose. As they find new ways that magic threes are used, you can add them to your ongoing chart. Remember there is no one correct answer as to what exactly a craft move might be doing for a spot in a piece of writing, only reasonable explanations and interpretations.

Homework Support

After noticing a craft move, students need practice writing, the time in class is never enough. Your students can try creating a new entry using a magic three, or revise an old one. Share successes and struggles the next day, articulating process and purpose for the magic three they chose to write.

Related Reading

Wondrous Words (1999), by Katie Wood Ray, page 177

LESSON 2: THE WHAT-IF STRATEGY

Components: Craft and Content
Mentor Texts Used: *Joey Pigza Looses Control* (2000) by Jack Gantos, *Wemberly Worried* (2000) by Kevin Henkes
Previous Lessons/Background Knowledge Needed: Thoughtshots from Advanced Big Pacing Lessons, Chapter 9

Lesson Introduction

The What-If strategy is a specific way to craft a thoughtshot (Lane 1993), that is, internal monologue. It can be used to slow the pacing and take time to develop a character by showing how nervous or concerned the character is about an event that is taking place or about to take place. My students will often use this strategy when writing personal narratives. I have heaps of successful examples saved from over the years.

Using Mentor Texts

I first found out about this strategy when helping my third grade student, Jackie, with her memoir about going to Mississippi to visit her grandmother. We were having a conference and she was asking for help in crafting time compression. She wanted to take the reader from California to Mississippi in an interesting time-compressed way and at the same time let the reader know how nervous she was about going to meet her grandmother for the first time. She was stuck. So was I. I didn't know of any mentor text that we could study where the narrator was nervously traveling from one place to another in a time-compressed way. I told her I would think about it and get back to her. "I'll think about it" can mean combing through all your mentor texts for hours or it can mean run around and ask for help. I asked for help from other teachers at lunch. Fifth grade teacher, Jon Marble, said he knew of something. He introduced me to Jack Gantos' *Joey Pigza Looses Control*. There, on the first page, is a child very nervous about going to spend time with his dad and he is bugging is mom by "asking a hundred *what ifs* about Dad."

> What if he's not nice? What if he hates me? What if he's as crazy as you always said he was? What if he drinks and gets nasty? What if I don't like him? What if grandma tries to put me in the refrigerator again? What if they make Pablo sleep outside? What if they don't eat pizza? What if I want to come home quick, can I hire a helicopter?

This was help that Jackie needed. We were so excited about this craft move we introduced it to the whole class for some inquiry work. We noticed:

- The number of *what ifs* is odd. (I have never seen an even-numbered one.)
- This character has ADHD *and* is in a nerve-racking situation, nine *what ifs* seem appropriate.
- Not only is the main character developed by allowing the reader to hear his questions for his mother, but there is also the introduction and some development of two other characters—dad and grandma.

My students decided they would use *what ifs* as internal monologue, a kind of thoughtshot. They used them successfully to improve the character development in their pieces. The following year I was so excited to introduce the strategy to a new set of students. I told them the story of Jackie and Mr. Marble and Jack Gantos. They all stared at me. Yes, we know about the What-If Strategy already, it's in Kevin Henkes' *Wemberly Worried*. I went to grab the book and there it was, the same strategy, written in first person in a third-person book with mice as characters. Henkes introduces the set with this sentence: "By the time the first day arrived, Wemberly had a long list of worries." Nine *what ifs* follow. Apparently this mouse was as over-the-top worried as Gantos' Joey Pigza character.

I wondered how I could have forgotten the *what ifs* from *Wemberly Worried*. I knew that book well. Then I remembered, in the previous year, when looking at Gantos' work, we had forgotten to use the inquiry question: Where else have we seen this? I don't know if anyone would have remembered Henkes' book. Certainly I thought Jack Gantos' book was the first place I had ever seen this strategy. Perhaps I had trouble thinking across from a chapter book to a mouse-character picture book. Since then I have noticed other *what ifs* used in other narratives that I had previously missed. It takes awhile to get really good at reading like a writer.

Jackie tweaked the strategy and made it her own (see Figure 10–4).

We were on our way to Mississippi to meet my grandmother. I started to wonder maybe she's mean or maybe she's a war hero, or maybe she's nice. I wonder if she is old, or if she is deaf, is she going to be a nut, is she going to pinch my cheeks, is she going to be a drinker is she nervous like me?

We were on our way to Mississippi to meet my grand mother I started to wonder maybe she's mean or maybe she's a war hero, or maybe she's nice. I wonder if she is old, or is she deaf is she going to be a nut, is she going to pinch my cheeks, is she going to be a drinker is she nervous like me?

FIG. 10.4

Jackie decided she wanted to let the reader know she was extremely nervous and she deliberately came up with nine *what ifs*. Notice that Jackie includes an introduction to her list like Gantos and Henkes provide for their readers. Jackie's is "I started to wonder . . . " You'll need to teach introductions, too. If you forget to teach the introduction element, your students might miss it.

Another student, Priya, used the What-If Strategy in her "Bear Watching" memoir. (See Figure 10–5.)

She decided seven *what ifs* was the right amount to use to pace the tension she wanted. She is missing an introduction to her list (I didn't teach it), and although her introduction almost seems implied, the pacing clunks a little without it. It probably would read more smoothly with an "I started to think . . . " or "I started to worry . . . " or "About a hundred terrible possibilities flooded into my head. . . ."

Other students have used the strategy in a simple, direct manner, often applying the magic three as well. Aoi was writing about a snow skiing experience. (See Figure 10–6.)

Aoi was one of my many language learners that year. She had come to our school two years earlier from Japan with no English. She returned with her family to Japan the summer after she finished third grade with me. I hope students like Aoi have a chance to continue practicing their English to keep the level of proficiency they work so hard to achieve.

Learning to read like writers helps your language learners pick up specific writing strategies, which helps them tremendously with their writing. Aoi learned to write in English far better than she could speak in English.

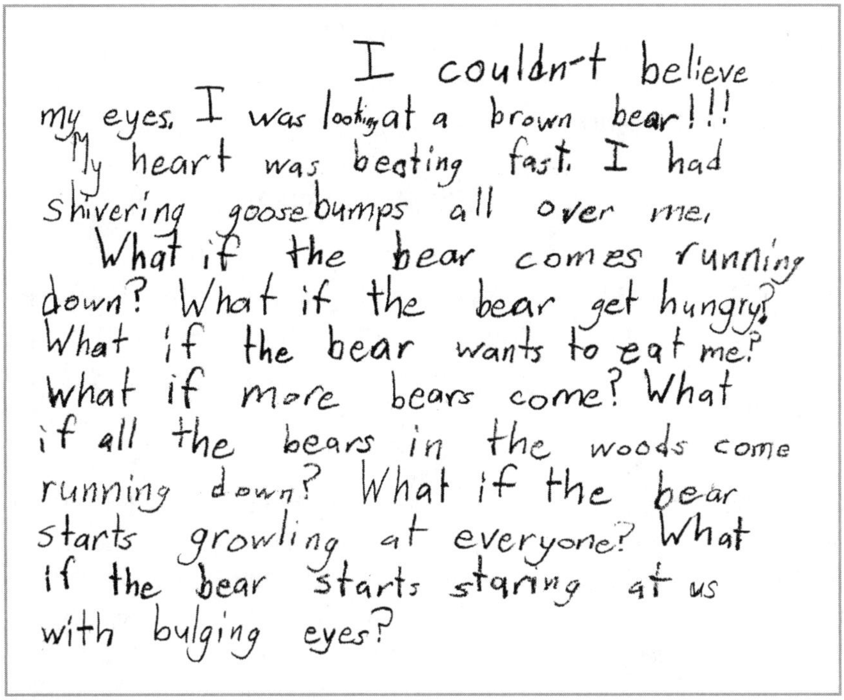

I couldn't believe my eyes. I was looking at a brown bear!!!
My heart was beating fast. I had shivering goosebumps all over me.
What if the bear comes running down? What if the bear get hungry? What if the bear wants to eat me? What if more bears come? What if all the bears in the woods come running down? What if the bear starts growling at everyone? What if the bear starts staring at us with bulging eyes?

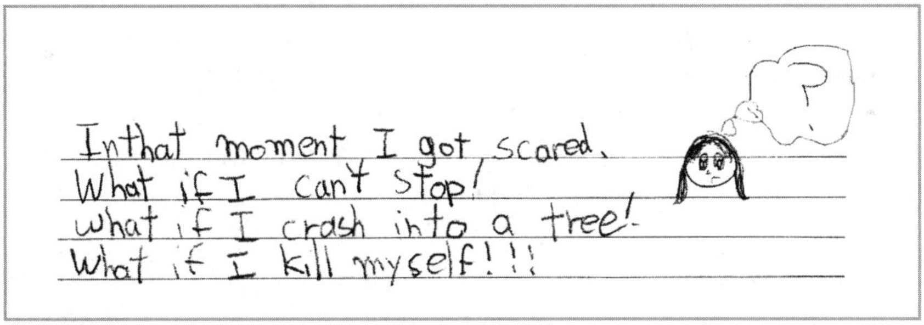

FIG. 10.5

In that moment I got scared.
"What if I can't stop!"
"What if I crash into a tree!"
"What if I kill myself!!!"

FIG. 10.6

Reading Workshop Support

After this lesson, remind students to be on the lookout for more examples of *what ifs* across the different narratives and reading levels in your classroom library. You can add examples to your What-If chart when they are found.

Homework Support

As always, extended practice with a new strategy will help your students internalize it, adding to their growing repertoire of writers' craft moves.

Related Reading

Craft Lessons (1998), by Ralph Fletcher and Joann Portalupi, page 63, "Inner Life of a Character" and page 93, "Internal Conflict"

LESSON 3: PACING IN PARAGRAPHING

Components: Craft, Content, and Conventions
Mentor Texts Used: *Fishing Sunday* (1996) by Tony Johnston, *Hatchet* (1987) by Gary Paulsen
Previous Lessons/Background Knowledge Needed: Previous work in paragraphing in expository text

Lesson Introduction

In my district, paragraphing is a language use and convention standard, showing up first in third grade. It's a very difficult concept in narrative writing. I gradually help my students construct meaning around paragraphing over the school year and by the end of the year I will see the beginnings of purposeful paragraphing in most of my students' narrative pieces.

I first introduce paragraphs in the context of social studies and science expository writing, simple report writing that we do outside of writing workshop and before a literary informational unit in writing workshop. We study mentor texts and I guide them to paragraph their reports. It's easier to learn the basic idea of paragraphing in expository writing of the kind we find in our science and social studies textbooks. I point it out, See, in this chapter about the Ohlone Native Americans, everything about their housing is in one paragraph, their food in another, their music in another. I can clearly show my students the basic purpose for a paragraph: it holds a central idea. *Scholastic News* is another place I go for mentor text for paragraphing. After I build a basic understanding using expository text, we dive into the tricky world of paragraphing in narrative.

This is so difficult. You completely have to lean on the reading connection. They must hear the extra pause that comes at the end of a paragraph, which is more than a period. Reading, reading, reading. Because, now that you are in narrative, it's not always about a central idea, it's about the pacing, how the writer wants the piece to flow to the reader's ears. You should be doing your best reading out loud voice while they look at the text you are reading. They need to hear the sound of pacing in paragraphing while they see it. It's really the immersion part of a miniunit of study. After immersion in the sights and sounds of paragraphing, then you go into your inquiry work.

There is one other consideration: is paragraphing really small or big pacing? In expository writing, I think it's big pacing because it's an important element of the organizational structure. Narrative is another story, so to speak. Paragraphing does provide those organizational breaks that a reader needs, but the pacing is tied more to the rhythm of the piece, the small pacing. You can decide to teach it as a small pacing craft or a big pacing tool, whatever makes sense to you. But do guide your students to see the work that paragraphing does to control the pace of a piece.

Using Mentor Texts

I like to use one of my touchstone texts, Tony Johnston's *Fishing Sunday*. Students need to be very familiar with whatever narrative picture book you choose to use for this lesson.

I begin by showing them the second page. There are just three paragraphs. The first two look more like what we studied in expository writing, so they can attach meaning to that existing schema. The first paragraph on this second page holds the central idea of getting ready to go and going. The second paragraph is an especially well-crafted physical description of grandfather, again a central idea. The third paragraph is a brief bit of dialogue.

I explain that paragraphing in narrative writing can be different from paragraphing in expository writing. Writers can use paragraphing for more than just organizing central ideas. Paragraphing can be used to control the pacing; it is one of the many ways writers have to control how the text flows to the reader. After looking together at this second page of *Fishing Sunday*, I pass out typed up individual copies of the first page. Here's the passage:

> Fishing Sunday, Grandfather calls it. It's the day that I hate most.
>
> Our house is as dark as a cricket. And still. Then I hear the shuffle of my grandfather's tough old feet.
>
> In the quiet he squawks, "Fishing Sunday! Fishing Sunday!" all excited like a silly sea gull.
>
> I groan, but rise and dress.

I have typed this example onto the top of a sheet of paper and then recopied it with no paragraphs on the bottom of the same paper. I like students to have their own copy for close study, but we'll look at how it appears in the book, as well.

We study the differences and we

- notice what the author has done to slow the pace—all those paragraph breaks
- ask questions as to why they are there—maybe because it's a sleepy morning, it shouldn't move too fast. And maybe the author wants us to have the time to really hear how unhappy the boy is. Have we seen this kind of paragraphing anywhere else?
- label "a set of short paragraphs" as a strategy used to slow the pace and give the reader plenty of time to consider the situation.

The most difficult thing is to envision and then apply. That will take so much practice, reflection, and discussion while students attempt purposeful paragraphing in their writers' notebooks, drafts, and revision work. We will continue, over time, to look at paragraphing in other texts; where else do we see our "a set of short paragraphs" strategy used and is it for the same purpose? I work on it formally and informally, whole class, small group, and in individual conferences for months.

I also like to use Gary Paulsen's writing for paragraph instruction, of course. His books are filled with great examples of finely crafted paragraphing for pacing. But it's likely I will not study Paulsen's writing with my whole class. If Paulsen's writing is a better fit with your grade level, be sure to have your whole class do inquiry work into his interesting ways with paragraphing.

I might pull a small group together that I have preselected, but I prefer to announce something to the effect of, "There will be a small group forming later to further study interesting paragraphing. We'll be looking at Gary Paulsen's writing. If this interests you, you are welcome to join the group." The students who are ready attend. We study Gary Paulsen's *Hatchet* for his masterful use of paragraphing. We study the long ones and the short ones and the ones with only one word. We listen to the rhythm of his paragraphing as we read it out loud and we spot the patterns. We follow our inquiry chart cues and we try to make sense of it all. Tough to do with third graders. But they do envision and they do apply.

They will need strategies to help them paragraph in their revision work. Before sending them to their writing to wrestle with paragraphing,

- I review the word *indent*.
- I show them the editing sign for paragraphing.
- I model for them how to paragraph a draft with some or all of the following choices that I have printed up on a chart as a help-with-making-paragraphing list:

    1. Read the piece out loud, listen for where those paragraphs naturally want to fall to support the pacing.
    2. Circle your potential paragraphs to easily see their sizes in relation to the others.
    3. Mark each paragraph with the editing mark.
    4. Take the piece to a peer conference and ask for help with the sound of the paragraphing rhythm.
    5. Check the purpose of your paragraphs; does your paragraphing make sense within what we noticed in inquiry work?
    6. Be able to articulate your purpose.

Looking at Student Writing

Carmen, an English language learner, learned the power of paragraphing to help her pace her memoir, "First Roller Coaster" (see Figure 10–7). (Her entire piece appears in Chapter 11, Language Learners and Reading Like a Writer.)

Carmen learned to use very short paragraphing to slow down her piece and create tension. She knew to surround her two short paragraphs with longer ones to create the rhythm she wanted. And she knew to use a longer paragraph to support her content that she was on that roller coaster and going fast, with no place to get off, therefore there was no place for a paragraph break, for her or her reader.

We went passed some rocks, some people and then I zoomed to the long line, my mom walked. Some people were yelling. I thought why are those people yelling it's just a little roller coaster. I will not yell.

Then after a while it was our turn.

I was excited. And scared.

We got a seat and sat down. Then it started, it was squeaky. It hurt my ears, my mom told me to cover my ears, the roller coaster was slow then it went up and zoomed down but I didn't yell. I was scared. I turned to my mom while it was going fast and shouted, "That was . . . scary!"

FIG. 10.7

Reading Workshop Support

Have students be on the lookout for interesting paragraphing craft in their independent reading. Continue to guide their thinking in whole-class read-alouds by giving them a copy of the text so they can see where you have that extra pause in your breathing for paragraphing. Discuss and articulate: When is there a central idea? When is it more about the pacing?

Homework Support

Students can use the paragraph editing mark and go back through previous writers' notebook entries with thought and purpose toward pacing. But I think it is a better idea to write a new entry with thought toward purposefully controlling pacing in the paragraphing as they write because when they know they are bringing paragraphing to their writing, they will likely write a different sort of entry with that purpose in mind.

Related Readings

After the End (1993), by Barry Lane, pages 122–123
Wondrous Words (1993), by Katie Wood Ray, page 174, "One-Sentence Paragraphs"
The Elements of Style, 4th ed. (2000), by Strunk and White, pages 15–17
On Writing: A Memoir of the Craft (2000) by Stephen King, pages 125–131

LESSON 4: PUNCTUATION STUDY #2

Components: Conventions, Craft, and Content
Mentor Texts Used: *The Worry Stone* (1996) by Marianna Dengler, *Miz Berlin Walks* (1997) by Jane Yolen
Previous Lessons/Background Knowledge Needed: A basic understanding of punctuation

Lesson Introduction

I think, like everything else in writing, punctuation could be endlessly studied. In fact, in my favorite conventions reference book, *Grammatically Correct*, Part Three: Punctuation, is by far the longest part of the book, almost as long as the other four parts combined. If you want to straighten out your em dash from your en dash, then I refer you to Stilman's easy-to-understand book.

After we do the basic four-day punctuation study in writing workshop, I then move our whole-class punctuation study to my word work time and my reading workshop time. We tackle more punctuation a little bit at a time over months, and I do start to see more complicated punctuation use appearing in students' writing, as they are ready to apply it—colons, dashes, parentheses. Over time, I guide them to the following understandings.

■ There are conventional uses and nonconventional uses of punctuation.
■ There are uses appropriate to certain genres and not to others.
■ There are uses that set the tone, the voice, provide the meaning and, of course, the pacing.
■ Punctuation paces a piece by marking the writer's intent for the rhythm and flow that he or she wishes for the reader; it marks your breathing. Take it out and the reader is not only lost but also out of breath.

You could choose to tackle more punctuation work in your writing workshop, depending on your passions, your grade level standards, and your students' needs. Again, I refer you to Janet Angelillo's *A Fresh Approach to Teaching Punctuation* (2002). Angelillo has everything you need for teaching punctuation in and out of your writing workshop.

Sometimes punctuation will be just what you need to teach more of within your writing workshop. If I see certain students are ready, I might pull together small groups to do this, but mostly I will do punctuation work in individual conferences as the need arises.

An Individual Conference: Looking at Student Writing

My son, Max, was one of my students in his third grade year. I was initially concerned it might be a bad idea, but if you ever get the chance, I recommend it.

Max was working on improving a scene in his memoir about his first time out on his own ocean kayak. (The parent part of me had to stay quiet, as always, which was especially difficult since I had been out there on our kayaks with him.) He did a lot of revision work, adding more and more detail to his one sentence about paddling past the sea lions. I only have the first sentence for you in his handwriting, as he switched to the computer for the remainder of the piece. Once Max started work on the computer, I asked him to save all his changes. You can see his first sentence in Figure 10–8.

When we were out of the docks and past the stinky, noisy sea lions the waves were pretty rough.

FIG. 10.8 *When we were out of the docks and past the stinky, noisy sea lions the waves were pretty rough.*

As a class, we were doing a revision unit, working to develop our snapshots. Max decided to focus his snapshot work on just the part about passing the sea lions and write more about the open ocean later. He wrote:

In about five minutes we were past the stinky, noisy sea lions all piled up on the rocks.

At this point, students were helping each other develop their snapshots by giving each other "gift questions," questions to prompt the writers' thinking about all the details that a reader would like to have in order to really see, hear, and feel the snapshot. (See Chapter 9 for more on this.) Max used his gift questions for more revision work. As he added more detail and the structure got more complicated, but he only had commas internalized to help him make it readable. That worked for awhile. He revised the sentence to:

In about five minutes we were out of the smooth, silent water, past the stinky, noisy sea lions, some big, some small, all barking over space, all piled up on the rocky jetty.

I remember doing a direct minilesson around this time about the unliterary sound of exactly numbered units of time that I was seeing in his and many other students' writing. He took out the "five minutes" making it sound more literary with his vivid verb choice.

We glided along the smooth, silent water, past the stinky sea lions, all barking over space, piled up on the rocky jetty.

But he didn't like the way this read, with so many commas, so he revised again:

When we were getting out to sea we glided along the smooth, silent water out of the docks and past the stinky, noisy sea lions all barking over space, piled up on the rocky jetty.

Pretty good. But there was one more thing he wanted to add: more sensory detail to answer a gift question, What sound did your paddles make? He wrote:

> When we were getting out to sea we glided along the smooth, silent water, swish, swish went the paddles, out of the docks and past the stinky, noisy sea lions, swish, swish went the paddles, all barking over space, swish, swish, went the paddles, piled up on the rocky jetty, swish, swish, past.

This version was very hard to read and he knew it. He requested a teacher conference. He said he didn't know how to help the reader read it the way he wanted it to sound. I asked him to read it out loud to me, so I could hear his intent. He did. I told him I heard the sound of his voice change with the "swish, swish," it sounded to me like he was inserting those parts, like they were separate from the description of the water, rocks, and sea lions. Then I told him when writers want to insert slightly different things or thoughts into their sentences, they can use a dash. (I made the decision on the spot that a dash was preferable to parenthesis, as he had inserts not asides and I stuck with teaching him just the dash.)

I sent Max to get a couple of mentor texts where I remembered seeing dashes but only in passing, I hadn't really studied the author's purpose. We looked at examples of dashes in *The Worry Stone*, but we saw they were not what he needed. They were used as a pause followed by further explanation, or elaboration. They marked off a descriptive element (Stilman 1997). It was good for him to see these because I wanted him to know, for his future writing, he could study other ways to use the dash besides what he was looking for today. Here are two of the examples we saw of an em dash in use to precede a descriptive element from the *The Worry Stone*.

> And in the evening they told stories—wonderful stories.
>
> Her hands tremble as she rummages through the drawers, until finally she finds what she is looking for—the velvet box.

Lovely, but not what we needed, so we turned to *Miz Berlin Walks*. I knew I had seen dashes in there, as well. I was hoping they were the "inserting" kind that would serve Max's purpose. I was hoping because at that point in the conference, if I didn't find what we needed, I would have to give him an "I'll think about it." The first instance we spotted had the same purpose as the dashes in *The Worry Stone*, but the second one was just what I needed to show him—dashes used to surround an insert:

> And then one hot summer eve, because I had nothing else to do—my best friend Frances Bird having gone visiting kin in Roanoke—I jumped off the porch swing and ran right after Miz Berlin.

We noted how the "my best friend" clause could be removed and there would be a complete sentence, just like he could remove his "swish, swish."

Max surrounded his paddling sounds with dashes, allowing him to "veer off in a different direction temporarily and then get back on the original track" (Stilman 1997, page 154):

When we were getting out to sea we glided along the smooth, silent water—swish, swish went the paddles—out of the docks and past the stinky, noisy sea lions—swish, swish went the paddles—all barking over space—swish, swish, went the paddles—piled up on the rocky jetty—swish, swish, past.

This is the most complicated sentence structure any of my third grade students have attempted so far. He never liked this end result completely, and he still doesn't, but the important thing is he was experimenting and he was learning about the work punctuation can do by studying mentor texts. Children need those independent learning experiences where they have the freedom to experiment without being told, No, too complicated, it's not going to work, change it to what I think is better.

It would not have been helpful, even if I had quoted from Stilman's book, for me to just tell him what to do, or worse, pick up a blue editing pencil and put in those dashes for him or change the structure. The most important learning point was to reinforce referring to mentor texts, where students can see craft and conventions making sense in context. I want my students to see me hunting down answers this way, too. I am modeling that habit of mind, that reading-like-a-writer process that they all need to be successful in their writing work. I want them to know when they need answers for their writing quests, our favorite authors will have them. And that works most of the time. But when we get really, really stuck in our quest toward savvy punctuation usage, I show my students that writers go to books that explain the use of conventions, and my favorite author of such a resource is Anne Stilman.

My son continues to read a lot and write a lot. Although he takes no help from me with his writing, I am just the parent now. Over the years I have seen his writing continue to improve and improve, through quality writing instruction he receives, and also, mostly, because he knows how to read like a writer.

Reading Workshop Support

Reading workshop is a perfect place to study punctuation, in shared readings and independent readings. You could include punctuation as part of your author studies, this is especially effective when comparing two authors with different punctuation styles. Flip through the works of your class' favorite authors. I have notice that some authors are partial to dashes, and some use none, some use punctuation conventions unconventionally and some never do. Every author has a style that shows itself in all aspects of his or her work, including punctuation choices.

Homework Support

Depending on where the student is in understanding punctuation use, have them either return to previous notebook entries and edit for punctuation, or have them revise an entry, trying out different ways to punctuate, imitating the work of authors that you are studying in class. Either way, encourage them to consult a mentor text for ideas or when confused.

Related Readings

Grammatically Correct (1997), by Anne Stilman, Part Three: Punctuation

A Fresh Approach to Teaching Punctuation (2002), by Janet Angelillo

Wondrous Words (1999), by Katie Wood Ray, pages 178–185, "Wondrous Marks of Punctuation"

LESSON 5: VIVID VERBS

Component: Craft and Content

Mentor Texts Used: *Come On, Rain!* (1999) by Karen Hesse; *What You Know First* (1998) by Patricia MacLachlan

Previous Lessons/Background Knowledge Needed: Basic small pacing lessons, basic parts of speech, and a solid understanding of what a verb is

Lesson Introduction

What we often see, when scoring student papers against a standards-based rubric, is the overall level of language will account for whether or not a paper meets the standard when all other elements are in place.

A study of vivid verbs in one way to raise your students' understanding of language. Precise word choice builds images for the reader. The reader expects that. Through your work in your reading workshop, help your students understand that they are able to visualize the images (Zimmermann and Keene 1997) because of a writer's word choice. As writers, your students should plan on helping their readers see what it is they want them to see.

You could adapt this lesson to anything similar to precision-in-word-choice work—simile, metaphor, adverbs, adjectives—any word choice skill you would like to emphasize. Your ongoing assessments will tell you what to choose. I decided to include vivid verbs as a sample lesson because verb choice is so important to good writing. There is plenty of discourse out there on the need to use vivid verbs in contrast to the discourse on overuse and abuse of similes, adjectives, and in particular, adverbs. We must be diligent about teaching purpose and know that having students randomly sticking gems and golden lines and luscious language—or whatever words are used for a particular part of speech—only serves to clunk the pacing by disturbing the flow of the piece. Where that golden line shined bright in a mentor text, a close imitation will simply appear as an inflated part of speech if a student randomly works it into his or her writing.

We need to help our students see, through direct lessons or guided inquiry, that beautiful language is carefully and precisely constructed with purpose. The writing reads well because every aspect of the small pacing is attended to. Vivid verbs are a wonderful place to start building this skill. But I have seen students have such a difficult time learning vivid verbs. Probably because the concept is difficult to teach.

Before I learned to lean on guided inquiry I tried a lot of different things. I tried making a chart with vivid verbs—plain verbs on one side and all their synonyms on the other. I found, as I constructed this chart together with my students, that I had to help them find the vocabulary because their synonym selection was quite limited. And since this was an exercise out of context and they did not have vivid verb vocabulary internalized in the first place, the chart sat on the wall and was not used.

I tried having students go through their pieces and circle the verbs, then consider replacements for them. If they could find that part of speech to start with, they were then stuck on choosing a replacement. Again, lack of vocabulary.

I tried directing them to a thesaurus. But you get some silly sounding words that way; the reader can see the author reached too far for a vivid verb and lost the meaning. Additionally, students might go overboard and replace all plain verbs with vivid ones, making for thick and bumpy pacing if not ridiculous reading.

I finally understood what to do. Whenever you have something that is difficult to teach, turn it over to your students. Let them do the inquiry work; they will learn and so will you.

Using Mentor Texts

In this inquiry work I guide my students toward two things:

1. Learning that it is just as important to know when not to use a vivid verb as it is when to use one
2. Helping them add to their verb vocabulary in a meaningful, in-context way

You could study your study stacks for vivid verbs ahead of your students, getting ready to guide their findings, or just let them dive in and you dive in with them.

Notice. Ask questions. Label. Envision. Apply.

First, have your students find the vivid verbs in preselected, pretyped texts or from study stacks, or just your touchstones, or whatever you decide. I like to narrow our focus and use just two or three mentor texts like *What You Know First* and *Come On, Rain!* When you gather together to chart noticings, divide your chart in two vertical columns. Write sentences (whole sentences) with examples of vivid verbs on one side, with a notation of the source, and write the purpose on the other. The purpose will be whatever you and your students decide the purpose is.

We noticed that if a vivid verb is taken out of its sentence, and looked at it, it was sometimes a very plain verb used in an unusual way that made it vivid, for example from *What You Know First*:

The cold so sharp it cuts you.

We noticed that not every verb is a vivid verb by itself. Why? We thought the writer wanted to give the reader a break, not make him or her feel out of breath from too much vivid word choice. Or, we speculated, if the writer used a vivid verb for emphasis and if they are used to emphasize everything, then nothing is emphasized. And when we tested theories (what would it sound like if . . .) by rewriting the text into the air, replacing plain verbs with vivid ones, we found we ruined the small pacing because the wording was too thick, distracting instead of delightful.

We noticed in *Come On, Rain!* that there is one sentence near the beginning with one vivid verb, *bullies*, and one plain, *climb*. Change the *climb* to *scale* or *clamber* and see how you trip on the change because you are still enjoying the first, *bullies*, and you want to savor it:

> The smell of hot tar and garbage bullies the air as I climb the steps to Jackie-Joyce's porch.

But part of Hesse's choice, vivid verb or not, is to carefully control the pacing. This sentence is from the slow beginning of the book, where everything is too hot to move fast. When we look ahead and find the beginning of the exploded moment, when the rain starts to fall, the pace has picked up and we can feel it in the amount of vivid verbs. In these two sentences, we noticed three of the four verbs are vivid:

> It freckles our feet, glazes our toes. We turn in circles, glistening in our rain skin.

Then, moving ahead through the exploded moment to the part where children and mammas are all dancing in the street, we found a particularly high-energy sentence, where the girls have grabbed the hands of their mammas, and we see there are five verbs, all of them vivid:

> We twirl and sway them, tromping through puddles, romping and reeling in the moisty green air.

We noticed as the pace slows down again, sliding the reader out of the text, the number of vivid verbs lessen, to about the ratio we found at the beginning of the story.

So why did five of five work? They fit together, work together. They don't fight for attention like *bullies* and *clambers* would.

And then we asked, is this a strategy other writers employ, increasing vivid verbs to help increase the pacing, the intensity?

I am not going to give the answer to you. Have fun with your students looking through your classroom favorites for the work that vivid verbs do.

A Breakthrough, Figuratively Speaking: Looking at Student Writing

I was beginning to see some successes. Joseph, in his piece "Enemies to Friends," tried it out. (See Figure 10-9.)

But even with all of our smart work in inquiry, it was still difficult for many students to apply vivid verbs in purposeful ways. It remained a vocabulary problem. To apply students need to first envision. And if they don't have a vivid verb vocabulary, they won't have a vision. I started looking for a different door. I found one in the study of figurative language.

He had a small earring glinting in the sun, and had eyes like a weasel. I raised one hand and then shifted my head slightly.

FIG. 10.9

One day I guided another inquiry in reading workshop. We have the reading standard: "captures meaning from figurative language." I decided I could work both sides of the coin at once. We looked again at Patricia MacLachlan's verb choice:

The cold so sharp it cuts you.

"Does the cold *actually* cut you?" I asked. Now remember third grade is the year where most students can developmentally shift from concrete to abstract thinking. But not everyone moves on the same time line. So I did get some arguing that, yes, cold cuts. But most of them got it as I continued to provide examples like:

Sunlight poured in.
She churned with anger.
Her words hung in the air
Let me fish it out of my pocket.
He was bent on causing trouble.

I followed each sentence with the same question frame: Does the sunlight *actually* pour in?

Slowly, verb choice skills continued to improve as students began to use the verbs they already knew in more interesting ways. We had started to notice so many examples of authors using the verb *pouring* figuratively, that it was a short step for students to apply the word to their own writing. Rayanne was working on the lead to her narrative about the "Drop Zone," a ride at our local amusement park. She had circled her verb *coming* and then revised it to *pouring* (Figure 10–10).

Dheeraj was working on drafting his exploded moment in his narrative about his surprise birthday party (Figure 10–11).

Shivering walls. I knew the figurative language door was working. Verb choice was improving among my students, taking their writing to a higher level. And in their writing futures, as their reading levels improve and their reading-like-writers-skills improve, I know their level of language will continue to improve as well as they move up in grade level.

It was a hot summer
day when I went to
Great America. The
people looked like a
wave pouring out from
their cars.

It was a hot summer day when I went to Great America. The people looked like a wave (pouring) out from their cars.

FIG. 10.10

And I can feel the walls
shivering. Then sud-
denly lights came on
my heart almost
stopped, then my heart
slowly got better.

And I can feel the walls shivering. Then sudenly lights came on my heart almost stopped, then my heart slowly got better.

FIG. 10.11

Reading Workshop Support

This is a great place to build vocabulary. Model coming across a vivid verb in your reading, getting excited, thinking about what it does for the sentence, paragraph, piece, where you could
use it, and if you don't know then write the entire sentence on a page in your writers' notebook that is dedicated to keeping vivid verbs. Notice I said *the whole sentence;* students need
the context, not just the verb, for vocabulary building. Model adding a notation of the book
title and its author so the writing around the sentence can easily be tracked down for further
study at any time.

In their independent reading, have them add sticky notes to pages that have vivid verbs or
figurative verbs to share with the class at closure. Students like to find them and they like to
imitate my question frame, for the rest of the year, Was he *actually* bent on causing trouble?

Homework Support

Have students go back through old writers' notebook entries and notice their verb choices. Are they all *went* and *was*? Encourage revision of entire entries. Ask if you could borrow a student's writers' notebook and model the thinking process for them first. Or better, model using your own writing.

Related Readings

6+1 Traits of Writing, by Ruth Culham, page 164, Exact Language
Craft Lessons, by Ralph Fletcher and Joann Portalupi, page 51, Using Stronger Verbs
Wondrous Words, by Kate Wood Ray, page 167, Striking Verbs

Other Lesson Ideas in Advanced Small Pacing

- There is a lot of small pacing work you could do with repetition. Go to *Wondrous Words*, pages 164–166, "Wondrous Repetition"
- Do a guided inquiry into selected narrative picture books for sentence length and construction and pacing and the purpose in content. I learned from Ray to type up the text into numbered text boxes. Each page with text from the book will have its own text box, like this from Karen Hesse's *Come On, Rain!*:

1

"Come on, rain!" I say, squinting into the endless heat.

2

Mamma lifts a listless vine and sighs. "Three weeks and not a drop," she says, sagging over her parched plants.

I used Hesse's writing for the vivid verbs lesson. And just look at her adjectives! Typing the text into numbered text boxes (for temporary, in-class use only, see copyright laws as they apply to teachers) makes whole-class or small-group inquiry discussions much easier. Picture books often don't have page numbers, or text on every page. With consecutively numbered text boxes, you and your students can quickly find whatever word or sentence or paragraph or page that someone wants to discuss. "I noticed an interesting vivid verb in the second sentence of text box five." Students can circle and underline and write their thinking on a copy of the text, important for inquiry work. I do buy multiple copies of my touchstones to have available in our genre mentor baskets for students to study, there is nothing like the original. But I don't want students writing notes on the pages of our touchstones. And for focus-on-text only inquiry work, I need just text, no illustrations.

Note: You will notice, when you look at Hesse's book, and many other picture books of different genres, that the text is often not arranged in standard prose format, that there is use of white pace. It's a stylistic choice that the writer or publisher or illustrator or somebody made. When I pull the text out of its narrative picture book setting for the purpose of studying just the text with my students, I type it up disregarding the use of white space. I don't want the white space to enter into our discussion—that's an entirely different unit of study. It would still be about pacing, as the white space gives me more pause then if it wasn't there, but it's more than where I need to go in my grade level to help them improve their writing in the time that I have.

An inquiry project like this, which would result in students producing a picture book with attention to placement of text with white space and in relation to the illustrations, could be done as backup work by any student who even notices this stylistic choice in the first place. And if I ever think my students have their writing under control enough—read: meeting standards— that we could afford the time to do a text-placement-in-an-illustrated-picture book study, whole class, then I will point it out to them and see if they are interested. But if they were ready, they would probably notice it themselves and ask to go there. They don't.

Other Lesson Ideas in Advanced Small Pacing Lessons

- Do a guided inquiry into similes; I like to show students that our class touchstone, *White Water,* only has two similes. I like to make the point that, as writers, they should be careful for two things: simile content has to fit the surrounding writing content, and too many similes is like too many cherries on your sundae. Yes, some kids will disagree with that metaphor, but I like to give them something besides the river metaphor now and then.

- Use Strunk and White's *The Elements of Style* (2000). It's been updated with a chapter on writing. See pages 21–24 for discussion on word choice that you could easily turn into direct lessons.

- Any other lessons that will support students' need in small pacing work based on what you see in ongoing assessment of their writing in relation to the standards or what you are passionate about teaching or what they have expressed interest in learning.

Language Learners and Reading Like a Writer

I remember my son lamenting one day, right around second grade, that something was wrong with our family because we speak only one language. His experience, at all of his friends' houses, showed him it is the norm to speak another language besides English: Spanish, Hindi, Chinese. And those were just *his* friends. At our school twenty-one different languages are spoken. What was wrong with us? my son asked.

Indeed, what *is* wrong with us? I wish I had a second language to offer him. I know my son will have to *learn* a second language, in school, from a textbook, and in a language lab with prerecorded conversations. He won't be able to *acquire* a second language because he is immersed in English.

Lucky for our English language learners they live here. They are acquiring English every day.

Sometimes, language learners arrive at our school on the first day knowing no English at all. I have had only two students like that so far, a girl from Iran and a boy from Korea. They wrote in their writers' notebooks in their primary and only language. It is most important that our language learners express themselves and if they can only do that in Farsi or Korean, then that's what they do. English will begin to slip in as fast as the child can manage. As teachers, we want to speed up the process, but out-of-context grammar sheets are not the way to go.

It is important to remember that all our students are language learners. Not one of them, including the "English only's" have mastered English. I have had English-only students whose English was worse than some of my English language learners. And I have had language learners who were quite weak in their primary language. Every child has unique, individual, language-learning needs. How do we address all of those different needs?

I assist my language learners the same way I assisted, and still assist, my son as he acquires his only language (so far), English. I concretely attach meaning to words. I casually smile and nod while correcting spoken grammar and expect the corrected sentence to be repeated back. I speak clearly and I adjust my level of language to the individual child. I sit with them as they learn to read, discussing pictures and text and helping them to attach English vocabulary and connect meaning to their own lives. I make the classroom community a welcoming place, including literature from diverse cultures. But primarily, I teach them to read like writers, because that's what we do, as a class.

I have learned something over the years: Teaching your students to read like writers is the best writing instruction you can give your students, all of your students. I see the dramatic growth from the beginning of the year to the end. I see obvious and purposeful evidence of the use of mentor texts in their writing. I see all my language learners leaving my classroom writing far better than they can speak.

In Part One, Chapter 3, and throughout my lesson chapters in Part Two, I have included examples of writing by English language learners that show the influence of mentor texts and the steps of inquiry. We'll take a closer look here at the writing of just two students, Carmen and Ricardo. We'll look first at an entire piece from early in the year and then one from later in the year.

Carmen

Carmen told me stories of spending most of her kindergarten year in tears, not being able to understand her teacher or her classmates. Carmen loved our art time, she loved to express herself in her beautiful drawings and paintings. Math was difficult, but she was proud of her growing successes in writing.

Carmen's piece of writing (Figure 11–1) was the finished product of a descriptive writing unit of study, done in the first few weeks of school.

In this unit, we focused on sensory detail and used the mentor text, *Owl Moon*, which you can see in her efforts at this beginning point in the year. This piece went through many revisions, yet her struggle with the language is still obvious.

Later, in April, she published "First Roller Coaster" (see Figure 11–2).

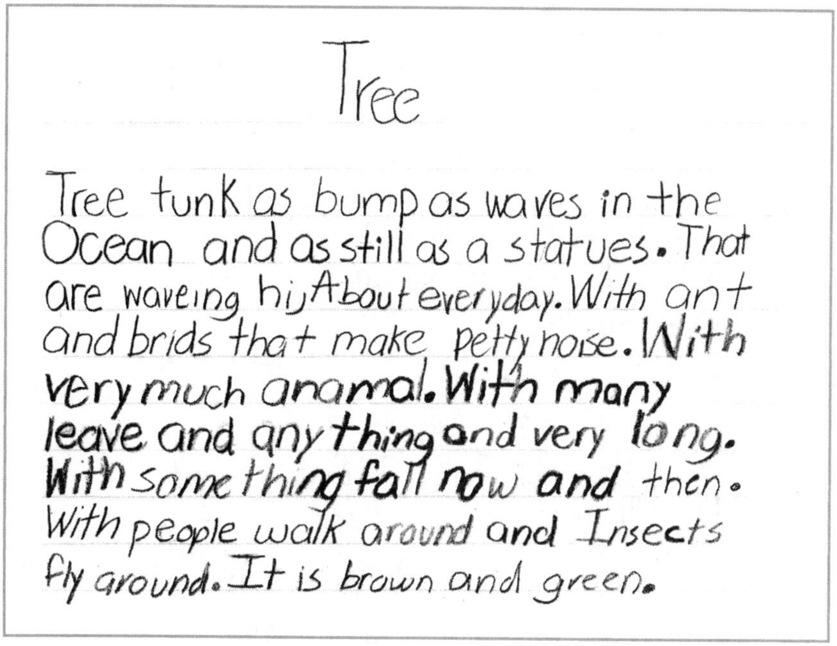

Tree

Tree tunk as bump as waves in the Ocean and as still as a statues. That are waveing hi, About everyday. With ant and brids that make petty noise. With very much anamal. With many leave and any thing and very long. With some thing fall now and then. With people walk around and Insects fly around. It is brown and green.

FIG. 11.1

Tree trunk as bump as waves in the ocean and as still as a statues. That are waving hi, about everyday. With ant and birds that make pretty noise. With very much animal. With many leave and anything and very long. With something fall now and then. With people walk around and insects walk around. It is brown and green.

Notice:

- For her opening paragraph Carmen used *Owl Moon* as her mentor text, and she added the sensory detail of smell.

- She uses short sentences and paragraphing for emphasis, like in *Fishing Sunday* and *Thundercake*.

- She knew not to get to her turning point too quickly, developing the arc of her story, controlling her big pacing by building up to her exploded moment, with her mom telling her "Later" every time she asks to ride the roller coaster. She hears "Later" exactly three times before she gets a yes, like The Big 3 we studied in *White Water*, and like the buildup to finding the owl in *Owl Moon*.

- She exploded her moment like in *Beekeepers* and *White Water*.

- She crafts time compression similar to *Beekeepers*.

- She uses the List Strategy from *Thundercake* to slow her ending.

First Roller Coaster

April 12, 2004

It was the middle of the day. My family was at Great America. The sun was bright, there was no wind. Somewhere people were yelling and the smell of popcorn and cotton candy was every where.

I was with my mom, my sister and aunt and cousins.

The I saw it. The roller coaster.

Then I thought, I wish I could go, I just need to tell mom. I asked my mom, "Can I go on the roller coaster?"

My mom said "Later." And I thought I know I want to go, but I don't want to be mean, like yelling do you want me to wait for ever, but I really want to go.

Then later we walked past the roller coaster, snack shop and the soda machine to go see a show. Then again I asked my mom, "Can I go on the roller coaster?"

My mom said "Later." I wanted to go! But I said ok but I really wanted to go!

Then I thought, I wish I can go, do you want me too wait for ever? We went to get ice cream.

(Continues)

FIG. 11.2 Carmen learned to write like this, including her conventions, from our inquiry work into our favorite narrative mentor texts, as you've seen in the lesson chapters.

Then hours later I asked my mom "Can I please go on the roller coaster? Please mom!"

My mom said "Later."

I said "oh." Then I thought, I wish I could go, I been wait for ever how much more do you wait me to wait! Then hours later I ask my mom again "Can I please go on the roller coaster mom? Please mom!"

She said "Yes, just because you've been asking the whole day."

I said "Thank you! Thank you! A lot Mom."

We went passed some rocks, some people and then I zoomed to the long line, my mom walked. Some people were yelling. I thought why are those people yelling it's just a little roller coaster. I will not yell.

Then after a while it was our turn.

I was excited. And scared.

We got a seat and sat down. Then it started, it was squeaky. It hurt my ears, my mom told me to cover my ears, the roller coaster was slow then it went up and zoomed down but I didn't yell. I was scared. I turned to my mom while it was going fast

(Continues)

FIG. 11.2 (continued)

and shouted,"That was . . . scary!"

She shouted,"Close your eyes!" Then it zoomed, then it slowed down. Then it was squeaked again, I cover my ears, It slowed down went up and zoomed down. Then it turned. it felt like I was going to fall off the roller coaster. It slowed down to a stop. We got off. I said to my mom," It was fun"

She said,"I am not going on that that thing again.

I said, "The turns are why you don't want to go."

She said,"Yes, it felt like I was going to fall off."

"Mom," I said.

"Yes," she said.

"I was scared," I said,

"She said,"But you didn't yell, you closed your eyes like other people. you were scared and brave. You didn't yell "Get me of the roller coaster." I thought a moment. Hey, I didn't yell like other people. I will never forget that day. and from that day on,

I will not be afraid of new rides and new roller coaster.

FIG. 11.2 *(continued)*

Ricardo

Ricky began third grade reading below grade level and with very poor fluency. I knew his word-by-word monotone reading, with no attention to punctuation, was not only hindering comprehension but would also hinder his writing skills. He completed the narrative in Figure 11–3 in September.

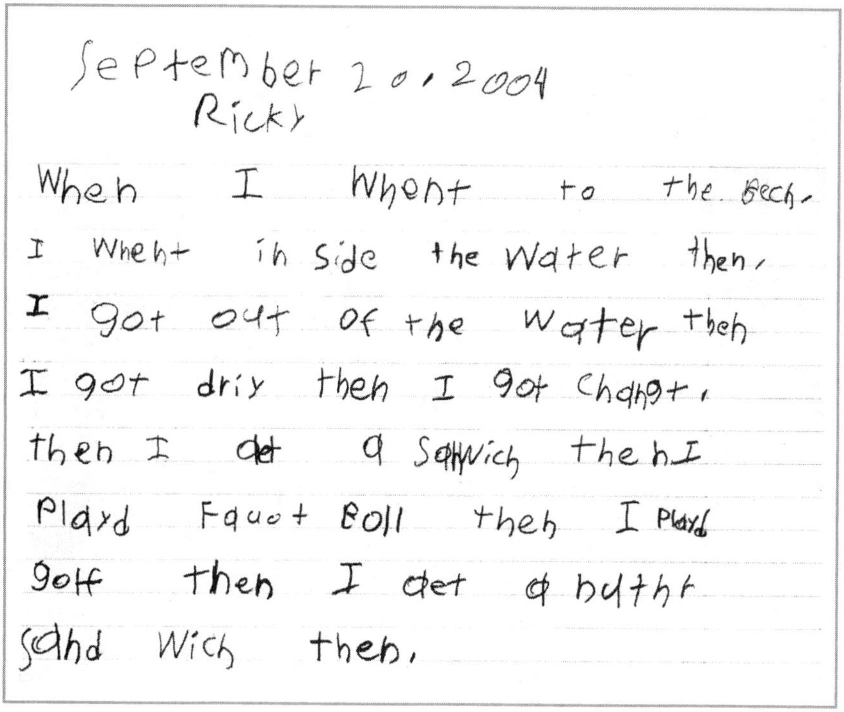

September 20, 2004
Ricky

When I whont to the Bech.
I whent in side the water then,
I got out of the water then
I got driy then I got chang+,
then I det a saywich the hI
playd Fauot Boll then I playd
golf then I det a buthf
sahd wich then,

When I went to the beach, I went inside the water then, I got out of the water then I got dry then I got changed. Then I ate a sandwich then I played football then I played golf then I got another sandwich then.

FIG. 11.3

He does show consistent control over past tense. He does keep to the subject of just being at the beach, but there is no story development, just a string of activities held together with *then*. And I am not sure if those punctuation marks are commas or periods, but either way, they are not under control, which is to be expected of a student who reads right through periods and commas.

More than anything, Ricardo needed the reading connection to support his writing. He needed to improve his reading fluency in order to create fluent writing. If he could hear the sound of language, he would be able to write the sound of language. We did small-group guided reading work. He read once a week with a wonderful lady named Ruth from the local retirement home. He practiced reading at home. And in class, he listened. He listened to the sound of fluent writing every time I did read-alouds. Figure 11–4 shows his complete narrative done in February.

In our writing workshop, I gave Ricardo no special language-learner instruction. Ricky learned, like Carmen, along with the rest of the class. My language-learner instruction is imbedded in all the literacy teaching I do, as I am working to help all students raise their level of English.

I was standing out of the pool. I heard splashes of water. I saw my big brother jump in then my big brother shouted out, "come in little brother." Then I said, "No I'm too scared." "No you're not. You're brave!" Then I wondered if I would swim or not. Then I jumped into the water. I smelled the clear water. I was drowning. I could

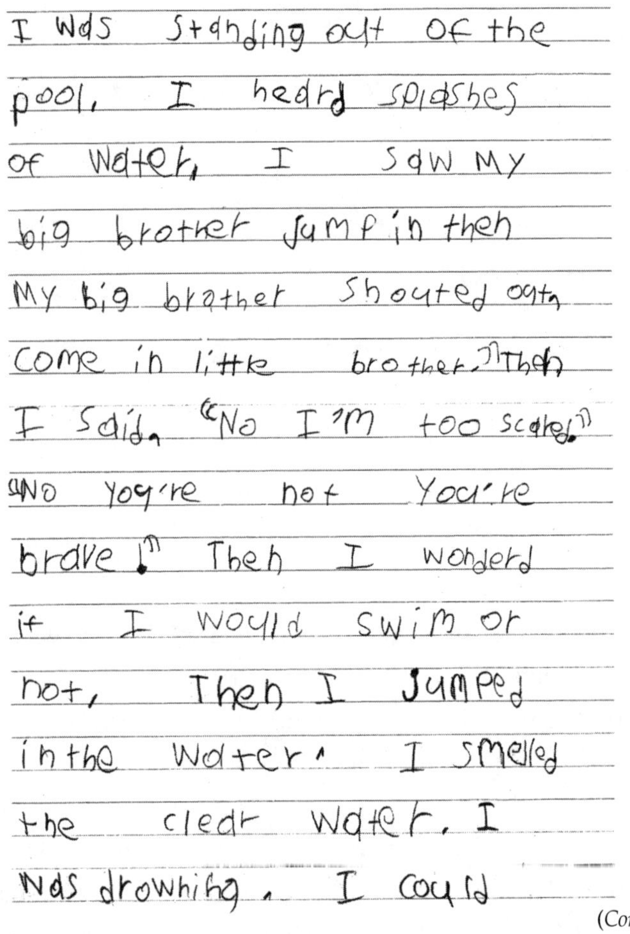

> I Was standing out of the
> pool, I heard splashes
> of water, I saw my
> big brother jump in then
> My big brather shouted out,
> come in little brother." Then
> I said, "No I'm too scared."
> "No you're not You're
> brave!" Then I wonderd
> if I would swim or
> not, Then I Jumped
> in the water. I smelled
> the clear water. I
> was drowning. I could

(Continues)

FIG. 11.4

Notice:

- He included the sensory detail of sound "I heard splashes of water" like the trains and dogs are heard in *Owl Moon*.

- He included dialogue to develop character and move the action like we studied in *Rotten Redheaded Older Brother* and you can hear the sound of *Thundercake* in "'No you're not you're brave.'"

hardly touch the bottom of the pool with my toes. I wanted to touch the wall but I couldn't. Water went into my mouth. I was scared. Then my brother saved me. He pulled my arm up and picked me up and got me out of the pool. Then I said, "That was the scariest day I ever had." But I liked how I swam and my brother was right. I was brave.

FIG. 11.4 *(continued)*

- There is an internal monologue in "Then I wondered if I would swim or not." It has the sound of the thoughtshot on the second page of *White Water*.

- "I was drowning" is his only three-word sentence, and it is purposefully used for emphasis, like "I was scared" in *Thundercake*.

- He built up the arc of his story to his turning point and he knew to explode it to manage the big pacing; he knew he needed more details like we had studied in our mentor texts and he asked for a teacher conference for help. (See Lesson 3, Chapter 7, Explode the Moment on page 92.)

- His ending combines the sound of *Thundercake* and *White Water*.

- He has marked improvement in punctuation control, which I noticed him employing directly after a four-day punctuation unit of study.

Both Carmen and Ricky made impressive progress because they learned to read like writers. They acquired writing craft strategies and the sound of language through our immersion work and explicit guided inquiry work that was always tied to the single concept of pacing. Guiding my students to learn to read like writers is what I have learned to depend on most to help my language learners.

For Further Reading

When English Language Learners Write (2006), by Katharine Davies Samway
Teaching Grammar in Context (1996), by Constance Weaver, pages 48–57,
    "Second Language Acquisition"
Becoming One Community: Reading and Writing with English Language Learners
    (2004), by Kathleen Fay and Suzanne Whaley

Pacing Across Genres

12

T he more we know, the more we know we don't know.

Who said that? Someone smart.

Occasionally, in this book, I have dipped into other genres besides narrative for pacing examples because I know in order for any writing to read well, it must be well paced, therefore I could find examples of pacing for you everywhere. I dipped into poetry and magazine articles and informational writing, advertising and movie scripts. But when I was first discovering what pacing is, I thought I should be thinking only about narrative writing. It was the only place I had seen the pacing standard after all. I thought it was the only place where pacing could be talked about, or found, or taught.

I was wrong. But I didn't know I was wrong until one of my students, Robbie, wrote a remarkable informational piece (see his beginning in Figure 12–1).

I know I did not talk about pacing strategies in our informational unit. Yet Robbie used small pacing strategies he had apparently internalized from our narrative studies. The piece reads beautifully.

We did, as always, look at mentor texts to help the class with literary informational writing strategies. To help craft introductions, we looked at many mentor texts including the passionate introduction to Jean Craighead George's *Look to the North: A Wolf Pup Diary* (1998):

> I love wolf pups. They have called me to Alaska's alpine tundras to lie on my stomach and watch them play. They have lured me west to my friend the wolf-trainer's house, to hold them and feed them from bottles. They have included me in their pup games in Alaska and Montana. I have howled with them in Minnesota.

When you compare Robbie's writing and George's writing you see the similarities in the start of the sentences. They both begin with "I love." George has "They have" three times; Robbie has: "I have," "I notice," "I am," "I buy." But

Flags. I love flags. I have loved them for as long as I can remember. I notice them everywhere, outside my school on a flagpole, in my classroom, in stores, on cars, at ball games and even in my Nana's and Papa's front yard. I am a flag Collector! I buy flags and people buy them for me. My favorite flag is the American flag, known as the stars and stripes. The Stars and Stripes have been around for almost 228 years!

—Robbie, from "The Fabulous, Famous, Fantastic American Flag!"

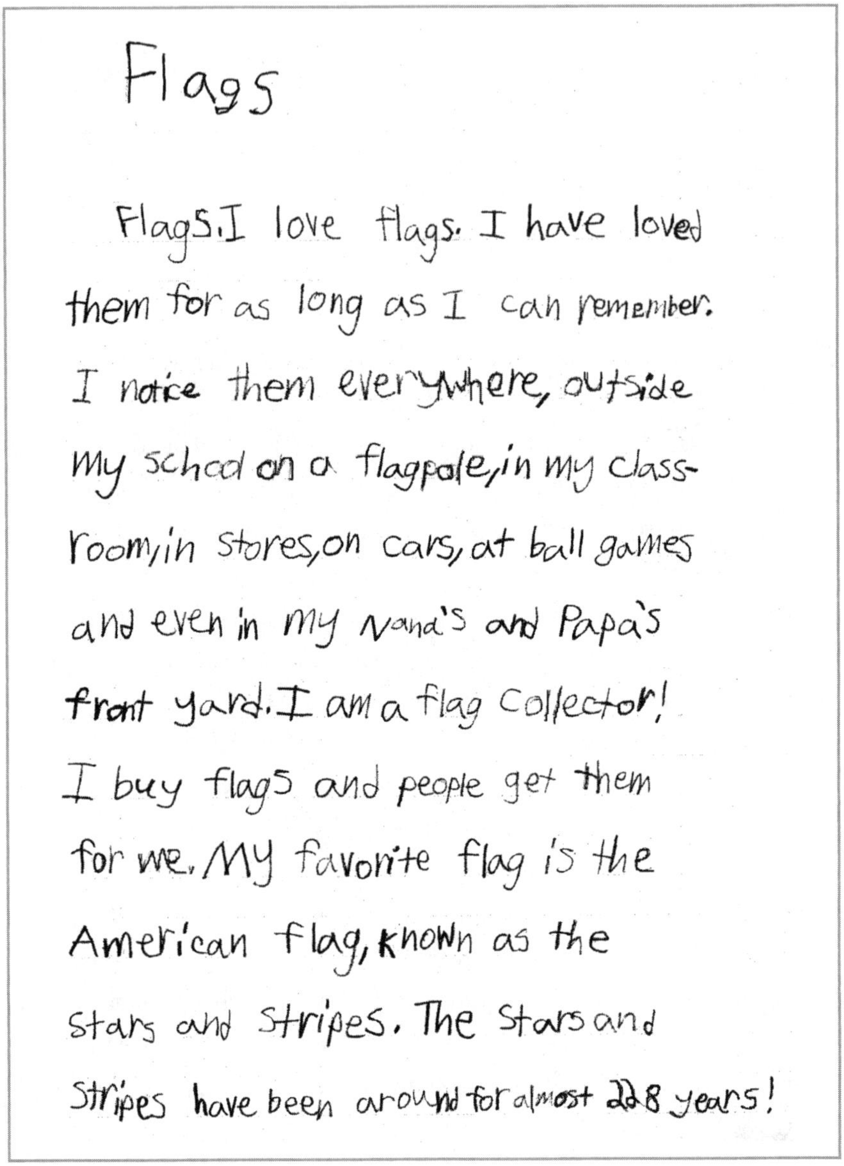

Flags

Flags. I love flags. I have loved them for as long as I can remember. I notice them everywhere, outside my school on a flagpole, in my classroom, in stores, on cars, at ball games and even in my Nana's and Papa's front yard. I am a flag Collector! I buy flags and people get them for me. My favorite flag is the American flag, known as the stars and stripes. The Stars and Stripes have been around for almost 228 years!

FIG. 12.1

then Robbie goes off on his own varying his sentence patterns with the sound of good pacing that he had listened to, studied, written and internalized in narrative writing that is showing up here, in his informational piece.

I noticed the rest of his piece is also well organized showing good control over big pacing: one heading and its contents flow seamlessly into the next from "Betsy Ross" to "Francis Scott Key" to the "Flag Today," "Flag Rules," "When and Where the Flag Flies," and "My American Flags."

We did study putting things in logical sequence and we studied using transitions. We studied spending enough time in each section to satisfy the reader. What I didn't understand was that we were studying big pacing work, with the same considerations for big pacing in informational writing that there are in narrative writing: sequencing, transitions, how much time is spent in each element, and so on. I don't know why I didn't call it big pacing at the time. I probably could have scaffolded more students' learning by adding, "Just like in the big pacing of narrative writing, your reader expects your piece to be balanced, with just the right amount of time spent in each section. Just like in the small pacing in narrative writing, your reader expects your piece to read well, so use what you know about small pacing in narrative writing to help you craft your informational piece." I didn't think of teaching these points until I read Robbie's piece.

I remember that Robbie and I sat down together when he was finished, and he wanted to write his reflective letter but he was stuck labeling what was so good about his piece. I scratched my head. Pacing was so entrenched into my narrative teaching, I just couldn't see it. "Well, let's see," I said, "It reads really well, it's so smooth, it flows, it has rhythm." It dawned on me. "It's well-*paced*!" (Lights flashing, bells, and whistles going off.) Embarrassing now, but true then. I was so focused on figuring out that pacing standard in the narrative context, that I didn't stop to consider that *any* writing that reads well is paced well. I don't know how I missed the obvious. I suppose we're ready to learn when we're ready to learn.

Now I understand pacing crosses all genre lines, is found in all writing, since pacing is all that makes the flow, the balance, the rhythm of the writing.

It takes awhile to learn this whole writing thing. That's okay. We can be patient with ourselves and enjoy the experience. The fun of it is—some new learning is always just around the corner.

Have you had a chance to take the pacing lens to say, feature articles? Have you noticed when and how much, throughout the piece, time is spent asking the reader a direct question? When, where, and how many quotes are inserted, how far apart are they typically spread? What's the balance in the organization, the big pacing? And how is the small pacing—the rhythm and flow—in the sentence structure typically done to support the tone, the meaning?

How about pacing in essays in general? Is it a gentle, thought-prodding essay, or an angry, soapbox essay? A skilled writer will control the emotions of the reader, the reader's breathing, through the pace of a well-crafted essay.

Since pacing crosses all genres, you might ask, why spend so much time teaching pacing in narrative? For results like Robbie's.

I always wait to do expository writing in my writing workshop after first spending lots of time in narrative (big and small pacing) and some in poetry (small pacing, primarily in specific word choice to support content). I know that my students' writing in genres outside of narrative will be better if I wait because they have had a chance to develop the components of craft, content, and convention skills that they need to support good pacing. Pacing skills they will be able to transfer into any genre. And if they have all that craft-through-pacing language in place, it will support conversations in the immersion and inquiry of a nonnarrative genre.

In the tie-everything-to-pacing teaching plan there are just two main ideas:

1. Pacing is what makes writing sound good, *any* writing.
2. You can learn how to pace writing well by studying it, by reading like a writer.

As we study different genres with our students, we will see universal pacing strategies in use and notice what is specific to which genre. If we have solidly given that gift—the gift of learning how to read like a writer—our students will continue to produce better and better writing through their school years, and likely throughout their life.

Postscript

I n my original research I found writing about writing by writers. I was reminded of our larger purpose: the connection from our writing classrooms to our writing society. When we teach the writing process and the craft of writing to children, we are teaching what accomplished writers do and know. Doesn't it make sense we, as teachers, learn more about writing from writers, past studying their work, past a few choice quotes about the process? Author quotes are inspiring, but shouldn't we be looking at more than just the tip of a writer's mountain of knowledge? Doesn't having a deep understanding in any curricular area make you a better teacher? I suggest to you that this sort of reading toward the discovery of the mountain can only make you a more confident writing teacher.

Some books on writing by writers that I have enjoyed:

Dear Mem Fox, I Have Read All Your Books Even the Pathetic Ones: And Other Incidents in the Life of a Children's Book Author (Fox 1992). You will get to know this gifted thinker and leader. Her joy and angst in being and in being a writer.

Take Joy (Yolen 2003). No angst allowed. There's a very funny bit in here about writers' work habits that I read to my students. She offers a magic word that is used by "truly successful writers," she explains. It's on page 61. The word is BIC: "Butt in Chair." Fabulous! And she has a great explanation about point of view through rewrites of the beginning of the three bears that also I share with my class.

Bird by Bird (Lamott 1994). A gift from a friend on my birthday, when I was in the beginnings of trying to write this book. Thank you, Susan. Lamott's book is a look into the world of writers with great advice on the writing process. Her chapter, Shitty First Drafts absolutely spoke to me.

On Writing—A Memoir of the Craft (King 2000). Besides being a fascinating account of his life, from childhood, always as a writer, this book is filled with pieces teachers can directly use in lessons. He offers great discussions on adverb overuse, unnecessary synonyms for the word *said*, a few bits on pacing (big and small), and all sorts of others gems of knowledge and experience.

I actually heard about King's book years ago, when it was first published. I remember attending a seminar where Sally Hampton (Carnegie Scholar and author of the "Learning to Write" section of the *NCEE New Standards*) was offering words of wisdom from the podium and waving King's book in the air. You must read this! she insisted. But I didn't buy his book. First, I didn't get it. When I thought of Stephen King I thought of supremely frightening movies. What would a horror novelist possibly have to say to me, a Disney and Pixar enthusiast? And second, I was too busy trying to figure out my writing workshop on primal level, how was I going to get kids to write about something other than aliens, if I could get my kids to write at all? Not to mention what to put on what chart when and what to say in a minilesson and, even more frightening, in a personal conference with a lost and confused student when I was lost and confused myself?

I was buried in piles of photocopied professional development help, working frantically, trying to meet my school's expectations, The Standards. But reading King's book and the others probably would have helped tremendously to comfort and guide me, like opening the windows to a stuffy office when the workload gets to be too much. Not only do we get a breath of fresh air, but we remember to stay connected to the larger world outside our classrooms.

References

ANDERSON, CARL. 2000. *how's it going?* Portsmouth, NH: Heinemann.

ANGELILLO, JANET. 2002. *A Fresh Approach to Teaching Punctuation.* New York, NY: Scholastic, Inc.

ATWELL, NANCIE. 1998. *In the Middle: New Understandings About Writing, Reading, and Learning.* 2d ed. Portsmouth, NH: Boynton/Cook Publishers.

BROWN, DAN. 2003. *The DaVinci Code.* New York, NY: Doubleday.

CARD, ORSON SCOTT. 2002. *Ender's Game.* New York, NY: Starscape Books.

CHRISTOPHER, MATT. 2000. *Skateboard Renegade.* New York, NY: Little, Brown.

CLEMENT, ANDREW. 2004. *Things Not Seen.* New York, NY: Puffin Books.

CREECH, SHARON. 2000. *Fishing in the Air.* New York, NY: Joanna Cotler Books.

CREWS, DONALD. 1992. *Shortcut.* New York, NY: Greenwillow Books.

CULHAM, RUTH. 2003. *6 + 1 Traits of Writing: The Complete Guide (Grades 3 and Up).* New York, NY: Scholastic, Inc.

CURLEE, LYNN. 2004. *Parthenon.* New York, NY: Atheneum Publishers.

DE S`A, KAREN. 2005. "Against all odds, student triumphs." *The San Jose Mercury News,* (June 8), p. 1A.

DENGLER, MARIANNA. 1996. *The Worry Stone.* Flagstaff, AR: Rising Moon Books.

DICKENS, CHARLES. 1964. *Great Expectations.* New York, NY: Scholastic, Inc.

EHRENWORTH, MARY, AND VICKI VINTON. 2005. *The Power of Grammar: Unconventional Approaches to the Conventions of Language.* Portsmouth, NH: Heinemann.

FAY, KATHLEEN, AND WHALEY, SUZANNE. 2004. *Becoming One Community: Reading and Writing with English Language Learners.* Portland, ME: Stenhouse Publishers.

FLETCHER, RALPH, AND JOANN PORTALUPI. 1998. *Craft Lessons.* Portsmouth, NH: Heinemann.

GANTOS, JACK. 2000. *Joey Pigza Loses Control.* New York, NY: Farrar, Straus and Giroux.

GARLAND, SHERRY. 1993. *The Lotus Seed.* San Diego, CA: Harcourt Children's Books.

GEORGE, JEAN CRAIGHEAD. 1995. *To Climb a Waterfall*. New York, NY: Philomel Books.

GEORGE, JEAN CRAIGHEAD. 1998. *Look to the North: A Wolf Pup Diary*. New York, NY: Harper Trophy.

GRAVES, DONALD. 1994. *A Fresh Look at Writing*. Portsmouth, NH: Heinemann.

HAHN, PAMELA RICE. 2003. *The Everything Writing Well Book*. Avon, MA: Adams Media Corporation.

HARRINGTON, JANICE N. 2004. *Going North*. New York, NY: Melanie Kroupa Books.

HEMINGWAY, ERNEST. 1987. *The Old Man and The Sea*. New York, NY: Macmillan.

HENKES, KEVIN. 2000. *Wemberly Worried*. New York, NH: Greenwillow Books.

HESSE, KAREN. 1999. *Come On, Rain!* New York, NY: Scholastic, Inc.

HIGH, LINDA OATMAN. 1998. *Beekeepers*. Honesdale, PA: Boyds Mills Press.

JOHNSTON, TONY. 1996. *Fishing Sunday*. New York, NY: Tambourine Books.

KING, STEPHEN. 2000. *On Writing: A Memoir of the Craft*. New York, NY: Scribner.

KRULL, KATHLEEN. 2000. *Wilma Unlimited: How Wilma Rudolf Became the World's Fastest Woman*. San Diego, CA: Voyager Books.

LAMOTT, ANNE. 1994. *Bird by Bird.* New York, NY: Pantheon.

LANE, BARRY. 1993. *After the End*. Portsmouth, NH: Heinemann.

LANE, BARRY. 1999. *Revisor's Tool Box*. Portsmouth, NH: Heinemann.

LONDON, JONATHAN, AND AARON LONDON. 2001. *White Water*. New York, NY: Viking.

MacLACHLAN, PATRICIA. 1998. *What You Know First*. New York, NY: HarperCollins.

MONTELEONE, TOM. 2004. *The Complete Idiot's Guide to Writing a Novel*. Indianapolis, IN: Alpha Books.

NOBLE, WILLIAM. 1994. *Conflict, Action & Suspense*. Cincinnati, OH: Writer's Digest Books.

PAULSON, GARY. 1987. *Hatchet*. New York, NY: Aladdin Paperbacks.

PILKEY, DAV. 1996. *The Paperboy*. New York, NY: Scholastic, Inc.

POLACCO, PATRICIA. 1990. *Thundercake*. New York, NY: Scholastic, Inc.

POLACCO, PATRICIA. 1998. *My Rotten Redheaded Older Brother*. New York, NY. Aladdin Paperbacks.

PORTALUPI, JOANN, AND FLETCHER, RALPH. 2004. *Teaching the Qualities of Writing. Portsmouth*, NH: Heinemann: First Hand.

QUINDLEN, ANNA. 2005. "Life of a Closed Mind." *Newsweek* (May 30), p. 82.

RAY, KATIE WOOD. 1999. *Wondrous Words*. Urbana, IL: NCTE.

RAY, KATIE WOOD. 2002. *What You Know by Heart*. Portsmouth, NH: Heinemann.

RYLANT, CYNTHIA. 1987. *Henry and Mudge, The First Book*. New York, NY: Simon & Schuster, Inc.

RYLANT, CYNTHIA. 1993. *The Relatives Came*. New York, NY: Aladdin Paperbacks.

RYLANT, CYNTHIA. 1993. *When I Was Young in the Mountains*. New York, NY: Puffin Books.

SAMWAY, KATHARINE DAVIES. 2006. *When English Language Learners Write*. Portsmouth, NH: Heinemann.

SCHUSTER, EDGAR. 2003. *Breaking the Rules: Liberating Writers Through Innovative Grammar Instruction*. Portsmouth, NH: Heinemann.

SIMON, SEYMOUR. 1993. *Wolves*. New York, NY: HarperCollins.

SMITH, CHARLES R. 1999. "Gimmetheball." In *Rimshots*. New York, NY: Dutton Children's Books.

SNICKET, LEMONY. 2000. *A Series of Unfortunate Events*. New York, NY: HarperCollins.

SPINELLI, JERRY. 1999. *Maniac Magee*. New York, NY: Little, Brown.

STILMAN, ANNE. 1997. *Grammatically Correct*. Cincinnati, OH: Writer's Digest Books.

STRUNK JR, WILLIAM, AND WHITE, E. B. 2000. *The Elements of Style*, 4th ed. Longman.

WEAVER, CONSTANCE. 1996. *Teaching Grammar in Context*. Portsmouth, NH: Boynton/ Cook Publishers, Inc.

WHITE, E. B. 2000. *Charlotte's Web*. New York, NY: HarperTrophy.

WHITELEY, CAROL. 2002. *The Everything Creative Writing Book: All You Need to Know to Write a Novel, Play, Short Story, Screenplay, Poem, or Article*. Avon, MA: Adams Media Corporation.

WILDER, LAURA INGALLS. 1971. *Little House in the Big Woods*. New York, NY: HarperCollins.

YOLEN, JANE. 1987. *Owl Moon*. New York, NY: Philomel Books.

YOLEN, JANE. 1995. *Before the Storm*. Honesdale, PA: Boyds Mill Press.

YOLEN, JANE. 1997. *Miz Berlin Walks*. New York, NY: Philomel Books.

YOLEN, JANE. 2003. *Take Joy*. New York, NY: Writer, Inc.

ZIMMERMANN, SUSAN AND KEENE, ELLIN OLIVER. 1997. *Mosaic of Thought: Teaching Comprehension in a Reader's Workshop*. Portsmouth, NH: Heinemann.

Index

Clements, Andrew (*Things Unseen*), use of short sentences and fragments, 114
To Climb a Waterfall (George), sets of twos in, 54–55
Close, Glenn, "ear" for good writing, 24
Close imitation, 85, 118
Come On, Rain! (Hesse)
    sentence length, 112, 165
    vivid verbs in, 162
Commas, overuse of, 157–58
The Complete Idiot's Guide to Writing a Novel (Monteleone), 10
Conflict, Action & Suspense (Noble), 8
Content. *See also* pacing strategies
    and choice of pacing strategy, 9
    communicating using pacing, 13–15, 19, 51
    relevant, focusing on, 82–83
    and word choice, demonstration, 164
Craft Lessons (Fletcher and Portalupi), 4
Craft strategies. *See* Pacing strategies
Creech, Sharon (*Fishing in Air*), use of groups of three, 146
Culham, Ruth (*6 + 1 Traits of Writing*), 6
Cut the Irrelevant (big pacing, basic lesson 1)
    background and introduction, 82–84
    demonstrating using mentor texts, 85
    demonstrating using your own writing, 84
    reading workshop and homework support, 88
    related readings, 88
    student writing examples, 85–87
Dashes
    introducing, 158
    in Max's narrative about kayaking, 159
The DaVinci Code (Brown), 82–83
Dear Mem Fox, . . . (Fox), 181
Dengler, Marianna (*The Worry Stone*)
    use of dashes, 158
    use of sets of three, 52
Detail
    amount of, as component of pacing, 17, 18
    relevant, helping student focus on, 83
Dialogue
    impact of, 17–18
    punctuation conventions, 102–3
    relevant versus useless, demonstrating, 101–4
Dickens, Charles (*Great Expectations*), 61
Direct teaching
    short sentences and fragments, 115
    for Snapshots lesson, 133
    versus guided inquiry, 70–71

"Ear" for good writing, developing, 25–27
Editing sign for paragraphing, introducing, 154

Effectiveness of writing, 66
The Elements of Style (Strunk and White), 59, 62
Emotional impact, as component of pacing, 7, 9, 113
Ender's Game (Card)
    pacing strategies used in, 14–15
    use of dialogue, 17–18
Endings, properly paced, 97–98
English language learners
    emphasizing reading like a writer, 38–40, 167–68
    read-alouds for, 26
    writing process, student examples, 168–86
Envisioning, as component of inquiry process, 120
Essays, pacing in, 180
The Everything Creative Writing Book (Whiteley), 8
The Everything Writing Well Book (Hahn), 9
Exclamation points, 125
Expectations, high, importance of, 70
Explode the Moment (big pacing, basic lesson 3)
    background and introduction, 92
    demonstrating using mentor texts, 94–95
    demonstrating using visuals, 93–94
    examples from student writings, 95–96
    reading workshop and homework support, 96
    related readings, 97
Expository writing, 152

Factrules, 56–57, 59, 63–64
Farewell to Arms (Hemingway), 103
Fast-paced writing, 17–18
Favorite books as mentor texts, 13–16
Fiction Factor: The Online Magazine for Fiction Writers, 6
Fishing in Air (Creech), groups of three in, 146
Fishing Sunday (Johnston)
    paragraphing in, 153–54
    sentence starting with "and," 60
    shotthoughts in, 138–39
Flashbacks, when to use, 9, 23
Fletcher, Ralph (*Craft Lessons*), 4
Flow, as component of pacing, 5–6, 8, 10–11, 12
Fluent writers
    attending to audience, 67
    effective use of pacing strategies, 11, 19–21
    reading like a writer, 24–38
    revision process, 73–74
    use of grammar, 56–57, 59–60
Fourth and fifth grade reading standards
    indirect reference to pacing, 10
    reading like a writer, 44–45

Fox, Mem, book about writing process, 181
Fragments, effectiveness of as pacing strategy, 63–64
"the Freeze" snapshot writing strategy, 133, 134–35
A Fresh Approach to Teaching Punctuation (Angelillo), 55, 123, 156
Frostberg State University English Department Website, 7

Gantos, Jack. *See Joey Pigza Loses Control*
George, Jean Craighead. *See Look to the North, A Wolf Pup Diary; To Climb a Waterfall*
"Gift questions" snapshot writing strategy, 133–34
"Gimmetheball" (Smith)
  complex sentences in, 122
  exploded moment in, 92
  illustrating story arcs using, 131
  sentence length in, 106–8
Going North (Harrington)
  long sentences in, 112
  sets of three in, 53–54
Grade level, and choice of example texts, 111
Grammar
  evaluating in context, 58
  and individual voice, 60–61, 65–66
  mythrules, debunking, 59–61
  and purposeful sentence fragments, 58
  resources for checking, 58–59
  role in fluent writing, 57–58
  rules, effectiveness of breaking, 56–57, 63–64
  and writer's craft, 37
Grammatically Correct (Stilman), 58
Great Expectations (Dickens), 61
Guided inquiry. *See also specific lessons*
  identifying pacing strategies using, 112
  for reading like a writer, 28–32
  value of as teaching strategy, 25, 69–70
  versus direct teaching, 70–71

Hahn, Pamela Rice (*The Everything Writing Well Book*), 9
Harrington, Janice N. *See Going North*
Hatchet (Paulsen), demonstrating paragraphing using, 154
Heard, Georgia (*Awakening the Heart*), 32
Hemingway, Ernest
  Farewell to Arms, 103
  The Old Man and the Sea, 62
Henkes, Kevin (*Wemberly Worried*), 149
Henry and Mudge: The First Book (Rylant), sets of threes in, 47, 52
Hesse, Karen. *See Come On, Rain!*
High, Linda Oatman. *See Beekeepers*

Hinze, Vicky, contributions to a definition of pacing, 7
Hull, Susan, on identifying main ideas, 83

Images and word choice, 160–64
In the Middle (Atwell), definition of pacing, 5
Indentation, introducing students to, 154
Independent practice, 32. *See also* student writing examples
Individual conferences
  teaching grammar, 57
  teaching punctuation strategies, 156–59
  using classroom metaphor during, 80
Individuality, and mastering writing strategies, 99
Informational writing
  importance of pacing to, 177–79
  as inspiration for reluctant writers, 41
  introducing paragraphing using, 152
Inquiry process, introducing students to, 118–20
Internal monologue
  shotthoughts, 138–39
  thoughtshots, 136–37
  what-if strategy, 149
  Zach's "Sorry List," 33–34
Internet, information about pacing on, 6–8

Joey Pigza Loses Control (Gantos)
  reading aloud, 27
  run-on sentences in, 113
  what-if strategy in, 149
Johnston, Tony. See *Fishing Sunday*
Jones, Edward P., 24
Just Me and My Dad (Mayer) and grammatical rules, 37

King, Stephen
  on revision process, 73–74
  on writing process, 182
Krull, Kathleen (*Wilma Unlimited*), 92

Labeling, as component of inquiry process, 120
Lamott, Anne, writing process, 181–82
Lane, Barry. *See After the End*
Lessons, overview of, 69–71. *See also specific lessons*
List Strategy (big pacing, basic lesson 4)
  background and introduction, 97
  demonstrating using mentor texts, 97–99
  examples of student writing, 99–100
  reading workshop and homework support, 100–101
  related readings, 101
Listening, as skill, 25

exploded moments, 92–97, 141
groups of three, 146
list strategy, 97–101
long sentences and run-ons, 111–14
paragraphing, 152–53
punctuation, dashes, 156–59
repetition, 165
sentence length, 3–4, 105–11
sets of three, 46–48, 50–52, 146
sets of two, 54–55
short, short, long sets of three approach, 48–51
shotthoughts, 138–39
snapshots, 133–34
sticking to the point, 81–88, 143–44
story arcs and elements, 128–31, 140–41
thoughtshots, 136–37
time compression, 88–91
what-if strategy, 148–51
word choice and use of verbs, 160–64
The Paperboy (Pilkey), dialogue in, 102
Paragraphs
  introducing paragraphing, 152–54
  pacing within, 17
Paulsen, Gary (*Hatchet*), use of paragraphing, 154
Personal schema, as source of information about pacing, 3–4
Personal writing, teachers'. *See also specific lessons*
  for demonstrating importance of pacing, 74–75
  for demonstrating sentence length, 109–11
Pilkey, Dav (*The Paperboy*), use of dialogue, 102
Plagiarism, handling, 86
Planning a Story Arc Using the "Big 3" and the "Big 1" (big pacing, advance lesson 4)
  background and introduction, 140
  the "Big 1," 142
  demonstrating the "Big 3" using mentor texts, 140–42
  examples from student writing, 142
  reading workshop and homework support, 142
  related readings, 142
  story arcs and elements, 141
Plot development
  role of small pacing in, 16–18
  story arcs and elements, 128
Poetry, and the craft of writing, 31–32
Point of story, helping students recognize, 143–44
Polacco, Patricia. *See My Rotten Redheaded Older Brother; Thundercake*
Portalupi, JoAnn (*Craft Lessons*), 4

The Power of Grammar (Ehrenworth and Vinton), 66–67
Punctuation
  commas, 157–58
  and craft of writing, 31, 57–58
  dashes, 158–59
  in dialogue, demonstrating, 102–3
  exclamation points, 125
Punctuation Study #1 (small pacing, basic lesson 5)
  background knowledge needed for, 123
  introduction and background, 123–24
  reading workshop and homework support, 125
  related readings, 126
Punctuation Study #2 (small pacing, advanced lesson 4)
  background knowledge needed for, 156
  introduction, 156
  reading workshop and homework support, 159–60
  related readings, 160
  teaching during individual conferences, 156–59
Purposeful Use of Dialogue (big pacing, basic lesson 5)
  background and introduction, 101
  day 1, useless dialogue, 101–2
  day 2, the function of punctuation, 102–3
  day 3, dialogue attributions, 103
  demonstrating using mentor texts, 101
  reading workshop and homework support, 104
  related readings, 104

Question-asking
  as part of inquiry process, 119–20
  as strategy for exploding moments, 95–96
Quilt metaphor for introducing pacing, 78–79
Quindlen, Anna ("The Last Word"), 63

Ray, Katie Wood (*Wondrous Words*)
  big pacing lesson ideas in, 144
  definitions of pacing, 22, 24
  inquiry process, 118
  on purpose of teachers' writing, 111
  short, short, long approach, 48
Read-alouds, 25–27
Reading like a writer (reading-writing connection)
  applying reading standards to, 44–45
  developing an ear for good writing, 24–27
  guided inquiry for, 25, 28–32
  importance of to fluent writing, 22
  reinforcing during independent reading, 32